SHAKING SHAME

from

MENTAL ILLNESS

Evonne Agnello

BOOK PUBLISHERS NETWORK

Book Publishers Network
P.O. Box 2256
Bothell • WA • 98041
Ph • 425-483-3040
www.bookpublishersnetwork.com

10 9 8 7 6 5 4 3 2 1

Printed in the United States of America

LCCN   2012913718
ISBN   978-1-937454-52-4

Editor: Julie Scandora
Cover Designer: Laura Zugzda
Interior Design: Stephanie Martindale

shakingshame.com

Dedicated to those who suffer and cannot speak.

CONTENTS

I applied myself to writing … in the same way that savages in their caves … painted … the ferocious beasts who prowled around them. They, too, endeavored by … painting these beasts, to fix them fast to the rock. If they had not done so, the beasts would have leapt upon them.

Nikos Kazantzakis
Zorba the Greek

PROLOGUE

To anyone suffering from depression or trauma, I offer the strongest hope. These are highly treatable conditions. Rather than a life of wasted days of misery, treating mental illness can significantly enhance the lives of millions. I know because I'm one of them.

One in four Americans has a family member or friend who has mental illness, and it's time we look in the mirror and in each others' eyes and talk more openly about it. There's no need for the pain of watching someone deal with it or facing it yourself. Those suffering *must* know this. Too many suffer alone from experiences that are common to countless.

What would our country be like if every American in need of mental health care received full treatment? How many homeless would find worthwhile lives? How much sadness could be replaced with vitality? How many suicides could be prevented?

Who will be the next American we allow to die on this doorstep?

PART I

THE BEGINNINGS

1947 - 1994

ROUGH RIDE TO GLENSIDE

For man never reasons so much and becomes so introspective
as when he suffers ...

—Luigi Pirandello, *Six Characters in Search of an Author*

How did a savvy and successful political consultant in his early thirties end up in a psychiatric hospital, then homeless, and twenty years later, dead at age fifty-two? What went wrong for Curt Mead, the small-town boy from Nebraska, who once lectured at Harvard? Was he really ill when he was committed to a psyche ward after he'd been at the top of his game? Or was there a conspiracy to silence him as he claimed for twenty years? Why did he live on the streets for months at a time?

It was December 1978, and our family had gathered at my home to celebrate my son's first Christmas. We were living in Aitkin, Minnesota, where my husband and I were publishing my family's weekly newspaper. Curt's political consulting business in Boston was going great. Eight years into his career, the references on his resume looked like a who's who of politics. They included JFK speechwriter and legal counsel Ted Sorensen; Boston Mayor Kevin White; Lieutenant Governor of New York Mario Cuomo; pollster Pat Caddell; and 1972 presidential candidate John Lindsay. Curt was interesting, enthusiastic, entertaining, intense, and full of ideas—the same old brother I'd always known and loved. He looked happy and healthy, dressed well, and with him was a beautiful and intelligent woman, Louise—an artist and writer.

It was the Christmas when my dad gave my brother the same book my brother gave my dad, Theodore H. White's, *In Search of History*. Dad's inside cover inscription to Curt read: "To our own 'young man on the move' who is making history not merely searching for it. Love from Dad." Little did Dad know that his lofty views of his son would soon wither and never regain the power of that time.

Several months later, my phone rang, and it was Louise. "Your brother is bankrupt, acting crazy, and holed up in the expensive Parker House Hotel. His psychiatrist called me yesterday and thinks Curt should be hospitalized. We think you should come here and have him committed."

"What? What happened?"

"There was a sudden and dramatic change. One day he was fine, and the next day he said he was being followed by the CIA and needed to stay somewhere with high security. He considered The Colonnade; it's like a fortress—a high-priced place where dignitaries and celebrities stay. His psychiatrist said I needed to get the family involved."

"Oh dear. Have you talked with my parents?"

"Yes, but it was hard because your father kept breaking into tears."

"What did he say?"

"He thinks he should go and do as the doctor suggests."

It was the week before Easter when Dad decided to fly to Boston to commit Curt to a psychiatric hospital. That would be tough for him at age seventy-one, and at thirty-one, I knew that this burden fell on me, too; I would have to go with him. Normally indefatigable and composed, Dad's voice was shaky and on the verge of tears in every conversation.

The trauma and drama of our task, coupled with a long travel day, left us drained of energy as we checked into our Boston hotel, so I suggested we go to a movie—get our minds off the gruesome work ahead. *The Deer Hunter* had won five academy awards the previous year, including best picture. I knew it was about Vietnam, and since Curt had been a decorated Green Beret in the Vietnam era, we could honor him by seeing this film. But Dad and I had no idea it was three hours long and included haunting depictions of war atrocities. Had we known, we would have chosen something else.

This was a dismal time, and while our tasks were hellish, they were not the horrors of war. This was not Auschwitz, for God's sake. We should have walked out, but in jet-lagged immobility, we watched until the end. We had tough going, yes, but others have had it much worse. In the thick of trauma, I grappled for a brighter side.

The next morning, Dad and I went to meet the police doctor. What a strange man and what a strange name—police doctor. Where I grew up in Nebraska, we had police, and we had doctors, but we didn't have police doctors. Curt's psychiatrist had made all the arrangements, so the paperwork took only a few minutes. Dad answered a few questions about Curt's mental health, grimaced in horrible emotional pain, and scribbled his signature on the document. I don't know how Dad's face became more disfigured by stress, but it did. I was afraid to pat him on the back for fear he'd break down—and that was not something a man of his generation, Tom Brokaw's "greatest generation" would do in front of his daughter. He wanted to be the strong model that he had always been—though it was clear that I was leading the strength parade that day.

Dad choked up and said, "I worked hard all my life to make things better for my family, and now I've signed a document that says my son is crazy? He was the little boy I taught how to run printing presses and assemble a Heathkit Radio, the little boy who read and questioned and dreamed—now he's officially crazy because I signed this paper? Oh, Evonne ..."

How can a father have the strength to do that to a son? As Curt's loving sister, it was no picnic for me either as I was clearly an accomplice.

The police doctor, Dad, and I hopped in a taxi for the Parker House, Boston's luxurious and historic hotel. Open since 1855, guests have included Charles Dickens, Ralph Waldo Emerson, the Kennedys—and now Mud Boy, the political consultant, a Beta Theta Pi at the University of Minnesota, and the winner of the 1963 Seward High School Senior Key.

There might have been those who were jealous, those who thought he was too cocky, too smart, as he dashed around in political circles. There might have been those who thought he was crazy and backed away, or worse—worked to bring him down.

When we arrived at the hotel, there was a paddy wagon outside—a little conspicuous among the shiny limousines. Two strong policemen joined us. The doctor had made all these arrangements. This was a surprise intervention and would be against Curt's will—that's why we needed the police. In legal terms, it was a Section 12; we were saving my brother from destroying himself.

When we arrived at his hotel room, the police doctor knocked sharply on the door. Suddenly Curt was there, incredulous at the unexpected arrival of his family, not to mention three policemen. What a surprise, what an ugly ordeal for him and all involved. His girlfriend, Louise, and another friend, Jerry, were already there, having arrived earlier to set the stage. Dirty dishes from room service were strewn about with about fifty books that he'd charged on a shopping spree. The topics were history, politics, government, philosophy—no gardening, self-help, or cookbooks here. Curt was puffing a cigarette, pacing the floor, and talking excitedly about running for mayor of Boston. The police, the doctor, friends, and family, we all had to work together to get Curt to the paddy wagon.

He demanded, "What authority do you have to conduct this unlawful act?"

The police doctor read the legal paper, "Wants to run for mayor of Boston and reads lots of books."

"What?" Curt shouted. "I can't believe this."

I piped up, "Curt, your friends and doctor tell us you've been exhibiting classic mania."

"Classic mania? Classic, smash-ic, Evonne. You do know I have studied these things a bit myself. Now, if you really want an example of classic craziness, you should read Antonin Artaud."

"Who?"

"An-tone-in R-toe," he spoke each syllable distinctly, as he moved across the room to a stack of books and pulled out a volume of the man's writing. "He's the Frenchman renowned for his descriptions of the anguish and oddities of depression. Susan Sontag wrote an introduction about him in this volume she edited. You *have* heard of Susan Sontag, haven't you, Evonne?"

"Yes, Curt."

"Well, that's good."

"My dear brother, with all your intelligence, can't you see that you are in the process of destroying yourself?"

"Oh, Evonne, you don't know the *half* of it."

After some discussion, Curt realized he was outnumbered and finally said, "Okay. I'll go with you, but I'm going to be passive and resistant like Gandhi, so you'll have to carry me out. This capture is not only unjustified but also illegal. Geez! Is someone crazy because he wants to run for mayor of Boston and reads a lot of books?"

Two of the policemen put their arms under Curt's and slid him backwards out of the room on his heels. I'd never seen anything like it before. His feet bounced across the plush carpet while Dad and I followed, wide-eyed. We moved quickly through the lobby trying to be as inconspicuous as possible; this was a classy place, and we didn't want to alarm the guests.

Curt, Louise, Dad, and I climbed into the back of the paddy wagon. There weren't any seats, so we each moved to a corner of the small floor. Once settled, Curt pulled from his jacket a small, ragged paperback, *The Stranger* by Albert Camus. It was dark inside with only one small window, but it provided enough light so Curt could read to his captive audience—though he was the true captive.

He began, "'Everything was happening without my participation. My fate was being decided without anyone so much as asking my opinion.'"

What a party. As the wheels of the paddy wagon ground through the streets of Boston, Curt continued reading, "'Surely [the jury] would not send an honest, hard working man to his death because he had lost control of himself for one moment.'"

When we arrived at the hospital, Dad and I accompanied Curt inside, and Louise returned home. The admissions man seemed cautious of this riled, red-haired, strong-willed man with wild eyes. Curt pounded his fist on the table and vehemently denied that he was crazy.

He sat erect and strong, his mood and muscles bristling. He stared hard at the man across the desk and shouted, "Can you look me in the eye and tell me I'm crazy? I can't believe you're saying the reason I'm being admitted is because I'm talking about running for mayor of Boston and read a lot of books."

The man's eyes rolled and looked toward me seeking help.

"Curt, will you please tell the man what he needs to know so we don't have to sit here all night?"

"No, I won't tell the man what he needs to know, Evonne! Don't you get it? This man is part of the plot, too; he has connections to all the others in this mad fiasco of deciding that Curt Mead is crazy. Well, not so fast, sister dearest! I have rights here, and I have my integrity, and I'm not going to easily let this man off the hook."

Curt did his best to offend and belittle the man with sharp, verbal blows delivered in startling and eloquent alacrity. He leaned toward him, firmly affixed a nasty gaze and said, "I'm going to make this little worm squirm."

Then, in a remarkable change of pace, Curt relaxed, chuckled, and said, "You probably don't have too many admission cases like me, do ya? Heh. Heh."

LOOKING BACK

You cannot teach a man anything. You can only help him
find it within himself.

—Galileo

I returned home from the committal deflated, depressed, and confused. After the two-weeks the hospital could hold him against his will, he was released and became homeless and out of touch with our family. I sought solace in recalling earlier, happier times and pulled out a file I kept of Curt's writing and letters. I found a birthday greeting he wrote me in 1968 when I turned twenty-one and was a co-ed in Minneapolis at the University of Minnesota and he was a Green Beret in the U.S. Army in Heidelberg, Germany.

Thoughts on my Sister on her Twenty-First Birthday

How intriguing (because of my own failures of achievement during the same stormy period) to have watched my salubrious sibling stroll with an occasional stammer, however, through adolescence into womanhood. I think back on the many instances when you came to my aid, of the permanent debt I owe to you, and I am truly thankful to have you as a sister.

For now, albeit apocryphal (for you were an adult long before I was), we both share the responsibilities of adulthood. Will you still need me, will you still feed me, when I'm sixty-four? For I can couch shame with a knowledge of the turbulence of my, at times, too analytic personality. How came you to weather outrageous fortune without as many pathological scars? What hidden resource do you have?

And so, I am both proud and envious of my understanding sister. Consequently, it is with a very smug feeling that I regard your entry into adulthood: smug because your emotional health does in some way reflect upon mine and because your ebullient manner will continue to be a source of strength to me.

Happy Birthday, Evonne, and thanks for being there all those times I needed you.

Curt Mead in his Heidelberg apartment, 1968.

When Curt completed his tour with the army, he moved to Aitkin, Minnesota, to become editor of our family weekly, the *Aitkin Independent Age*. His editorship in early 1971 was a golden time for the *Age*—a brief Camelot—during my family's thirty-three-year ownership. Curt was full of spunk, commitment, and ideas for building a better world. He was lucky, at age twenty-five, to have the platform of a small-town newspaper.

I found newspaper clippings of some of the pieces he produced as editor. He wrote powerfully and brought a literary excellence to the pages perhaps not seen before or since—quoting Aristotle, Wordsworth, T. S. Eliot, John Updike, Michael Harrington, and others. He wrote of the "timeless problems of war, poverty and personal disillusionment" and described "a vitality in living that was slipping away from our culture."

When President Richard Nixon's Vice President Spiro Agnew referred to the media as "nattering nabobs of negativity" and "an effete corps of impudent snobs," Curt skewered him in an *Age* editorial. He wrote, "Woven into the tangled flamboyancy of that mass of blustery locution which has become the rhetoric of Vice President Agnew, is a political cynicism which is both reprehensible and disheartening."

During Curt's editorship, he wrote some pieces that could easily be a part of Garrison Keillor's Lake Wobegon script. I've always believed that Aitkin

Curt Mead in 1969 as a Green Beret.

is a town that Keillor uses as one of the models for Lake Wobegon. There are just too many similarities for it not to be so. On one of those slow-news weeks that cause small-town editors to scurry, Curt created stories from bits of trivia, like the menu at the local lunch counter. People loved the fun and chatter this piece caused:

> Patrons of Ziske's Nationally Acclaimed Restaurant Exceptionale were bemusedly startled last week when Swedish Chow Mein was added to the usual noontime fare. Explained Maitre Di [sic] and head cook Gladys Woodrow, "We named it Swedish Chow Mein because we serve more Swedes than Chinamen." Head dishwasher Chuck Ziske said the recipe is the best kept secret in Aitkin County and is secure in the Ziske vault which is guarded by four ferocious timber wolves.
>
> But the question on the minds of most patrons this week was, "Where can the Ziske menu go after Swedish Chow Mein? To what new heights of home kitchen wizardry can the chefs now arise? Norwegian Lasagna? Finnish Enchiladas?

After a few months in Aitkin, Curt set his sights on politics and, in the spring of 1970, landed the job of press secretary for Earl Craig's unsuccessful run against Hubert Humphrey to be the DFL candidate for the U.S. Senate. Craig had become a mentor to Curt in 1963 when they became friends at the University of Minnesota. Before Craig launched his campaign, he sought reactions of a number of people, including Curt. Here's my brother's reply:

Dear Mr. Craig:

I have before me your letter of March 5, in which you solicit reactions to your proposed impending candidacy for the United States Senate. Having once served as a writer for a Four Star General in the US Army in Europe, I am intimately aware of the vagaries of the importance for the correct image that must be projected to become a member of that august body. L. Mendel Rivers is a man who comes to mind as an example of the quality of men currently serving our country. Rivers is, as you may know, chairman of the important House Armed Services Committee. I had the pleasure of meeting Mr. Rivers when I served in Europe. When he arrived at Frankfurt AFB, he was so drunk that he had to be escorted off the plane, and when I shook his hand, he reeked of liquor.

But, of course, that is beside the point.

In response to your query, however, let me say that I for one, have a Nikon and about 1000 unexposed negatives and about 1000 unexposed ideas to get your name one hell of a lot of exposure out in the "hustings," as I believe you city slickers call it, and I, just one voice in the wilderness, scream to you, Mr. Earl D. Craig, Jr., "Let's go get 'em."

Damn the torpedoes as well as the slings and arrows of outrageous fortune to say nothing of the coming of the gentle night, and I close with the urgency of T. S. Eliot:

"Do I dare disturb the universe?"

Curt

And I found a beautiful piece he wrote our mother when he was twenty-two and she turned sixty.

To My Mother on Her Birthday
December 18, 1967

To be loved by many and to love many
Is to never die, is to live purely
Never to lack for noble company.

Through sometimes clouded eyes
I see her, behind me, in front of me, beside me
Helping me grasp the world.
Loving many as she has done
So many guarding a part of her in themselves
As I do now.

Unhooded eyes, sparkling like fire
That must have warmed a cold farmhouse years before
Warm me.

She marks another year, alone
Perhaps a glass of wine before bed
None of the many to attend.

None to rise up, lift a glass to her
To gaze kindly at her face
None to express the thanks for the many.

Except her son, who far away
Sits muted, speaking with his fingers on a keyboard
Halting, stumbling through words not sufficient
Thoughts not enough refined
To speak clearly the emotions which impel him to write.

To rise up and scream to the world
His undying devotion
To speak for the many loved by her, who love her.

In March 1970, I became the first person in my family to graduate from college. Though eager to try my new skills, I couldn't find work so spent spring quarter in graduate school and ended up making one the best decisions of my life. Reading the *Minnesota Daily* one day, I spotted an ad for a one-way ticket to London for $250. Curt had recently returned from Heidelberg and had Minneapolis friends still there, Mary and Jim Conover, who would help me find a job and a place to live. I bought the ticket, Erich Fromm's *Europe on $5 a Day*, and flew off to

Curt Mead

an unknown destiny. The next year and a half was magical. I rented a small room in Heidelberg for $12 a month, worked in the admissions office at the University of Maryland European Division, and met and, a year later, married an American G.I.

While I was in Europe, Curt was energized and inspired to change the world—as many who grew up in the sixties were. He was among seventy-five volunteers in a national program called "Registration Summer," an effort to get the newly enfranchised young people registered for the 1972 presidential election. The twenty-sixth amendment passed in 1971 that allowed eighteen-, nineteen-, and twenty-year-olds the right to vote, and Curt was sent to communities to train people how to register voters.

When twenty-seven thousand people gathered in one of the largest antiwar rallies in Minnesota on May 23, 1971, my brother was heavily involved in making that happen. He helped recruit participants from forty-four colleges and universities, thirty-eight area high schools, and a network of political and peace organizations throughout the state.

Speakers included John Kerry, Al Lowenstein (former New York congressman) and Mrs. Richard Walsh, a Minneapolis mother of five whose husband had been shot down in Vietnam and was presumed to be a POW.

This was the beginning of the computerization of politics as people learned to use technology to mobilize citizens. Data from attendees was keypunched onto paper cards and then transferred to magnetic tape. Peter Nicholson, assistant professor in the Department of Computer Sciences at the University of Minnesota, coordinated the compilation and said, "With such an information bank it will be possible to obtain almost instantaneously the names of people in particular districts willing to work for antiwar candidates." Planners said, "No attempt has ever been made to computerize the myriad peace organizations that have spawned in Minnesota."

The next month, Curt organized youth voter registration programs and wrote press releases in Oshkosh, Wisconsin, and in July did the same in Long Island, New York. National anti-war strategists saw registration of the newly enfranchised youth, whose rejection of the war was almost universal, as an effective tactic to increase Congressional opposition to the war. At the New York rally, speakers included Bella Abzug, Paul McCloskey, Al Lowenstein, Michael Harrington, John Kerry, and Peter Yarrow. Curt organized a similar campaign to register young voters in Lincoln, Nebraska, where speakers included conservative political columnist William Buckley and New York Mayor John Lindsay. Curt thrived in the excitement of building a better America through the political process. He was a dreamer and sometimes dreamed expansively. He wanted to change the system by getting honest people elected to office.

In January 1972, Curt was sent to Tucson by John Lindsay's presidential campaign to open a campaign office just a few weeks before the caucus. The *Tucson Citizen* featured a large ponderous portrait of Curt with the story, "Lindsay Tucson Start Was Arduous Struggle."

In Lindsay lather – Curt Mead hurdles problems for New York Mayor Lindsay.
Tucson Citizen photo, reprinted with permission.

Staff writer Asa Bushnell wrote, "Launching John Lindsay's presidential campaign in Tucson has been an arduous, uphill struggle … Lindsay's decision to include Tucson in his plans came as part of an eleventh-hour strategy according to bewitched, bothered and bearded Curt Mead, his majordomo for Tucson." (Lindsay placed second among seven candidates, with Ed Muskie winning.)

In September 1972, Curt wrote:

> My job for the City of New York [in Mayor Lindsay's office] is interesting. I'm finding my army experience helpful in dealing with the bureaucracy, roughly the same size as the army in Europe, some 350,000 city employees. I went to Boston on Friday to talk with the folks at Martilla. [Martilla, Payne, Kiley and Thorne was Boston's leading political shop according to a 2004 *New York Times* report.] The firm will be running mayoral campaigns in Detroit, Houston, Los Angeles, and perhaps New York this year. They offered me a position for several thousand dollars more than I'm making now, but there would a great deal of travel. It's risky because it all depends on reputation, which is good for them right now, having won four of the five races they ran last fall.

When Curt made a bid in 1975 to buy the *Phoenix* newspaper in Boston, his references included Boston's Mayor Kevin White; David Cohen, the national president of Common Cause; and Robert Morgenthau, U.S. attorney, who developed a reputation as an effective opponent of organized crime, tax-fraud, corruption, and white-collar crime. Curt also had worked for Sen. Thomas Eagleton, George McGovern's vice presidential running mate in the 1972 election until the media reported that Eagleton had received electric shock treatment for depression and was forced to step down. Curt had also worked in the Minnesota campaign of Lt. Gov. Rudy Perpich and the former New York Rep. Allard Lowenstein.

In 1975, Curt had an experience that was probably the pinnacle of his career when he lectured at Harvard's John F. Kennedy School of Government. He spoke at a seminar on Transition and Leadership for Newly-Elected Mayors from throughout the country. Seminar Coordinator Ira Jackson wrote to Curt following the program, "Reactions to your presentation were extremely favorable. It has been a pleasure to work with you."

~ ~ ~

When my husband completed his army tour, my dad invited us to publish my family newspaper in Seward. Most weeklies in those days were owned and run by families, not big corporations. Many were mom-and-pop shops, but the man was always the publisher. At that time in Nebraska, 1972, and throughout the country, there were few women publishers. Therefore, it was rather revolutionary for my father to give us the title of co-publishers. While I was proud to follow in his footsteps, I was astounded when he set my husband's salary higher than mine because "a husband should earn more than his wife." I winced in disbelief of this incredulous news. How could my own father make this terrible transgression? Later I learned that the federal Equal Pay Act of 1963, which requires equal pay for equal work, had been in effect nine years. How could my father have been ignorant of that? I could have sued him and won but that didn't occur to me. That was the last thing I'd do to the man whose attention and approval I nearly always sought.

After working long hours, week after week, for three years, my husband and I decided to stretch our wings and leave our secure life in Seward. It would have been easy for us to spend the rest of our lives in that routine, but we were burned out with the round-the-clock demands of a weekly newspaper. It was 1975, and we were twenty-eight; we'd won top awards in the state press contests every year and even second place in a national contest. It was obvious we could do this the rest of our lives, but we were young and wanted new challenges. We sold our five-bedroom home and much of our belongings and went on (what turned out to be) a five-month camping and backpacking trip in the Pacific Northwest. While contemplating what to do with our lives, we ended up having some of the best times of our lives.

By fall, it became too cold for camping so we holed up in a Eugene, Oregon, motel, looking for work by reading the want ads. I spotted an opening for an advertising account executive at the *Bulletin,* the paper in Bend, Oregon—the innovative and family-owned daily run by the bright, colorful, and shrewd Bob Chandler. Up until that time, there had been no women in the display-ad sales force, and all businesses were highly male-dominated. Working at the *Bulletin* was my first job at a daily newspaper, and that was big potatoes to a small-town gal like me who had, heretofore, worked only at my family-owned weeklies. After a blissful year in sunny Bend, my husband wanted to return to college, and we moved to Portland. My goal was to work for one of the two strong dailies in the region, the *Oregonian* or the *Columbian*, across the river in Vancouver, Washington. Both had reputations as great places to work and were purveyors of some of the best journalism in the Northwest. Each had lots of people clamoring for positions, and I got in line.

In the meantime, I took a job at a downtown weekly fluff paper, as I called it. The focus was fashion, fun, and frivolity. It was interesting to meet the downtown Portland merchants, but I was revolted by a newspaper with no editorial page or news of consequence. The stories were about the people to whom we were selling advertising and, in my experience, there had always been an immutable line between news and advertising. But this wasn't a traditional newspaper, and I was a long way from my Nebraska roots. The fluff paper bent the rules I had always held sacred, and it sickened me. I'll never forget my disgust when I had to interview and write about a lady whose business was gluing on fake fingernails. How I struggled, pretending that this was the most important thing a woman could do for herself. The larger dilemma was finding something more meaningful to do with my life. I wanted to expose injustice and wrongdoing; instead, I was groping for words to describe bogus excitement. Luckily, I soon landed a job at the *Columbian* and shortly after that became pregnant. About that time, Curt wrote on his business letterhead, Mead & Bender Communications (12 Arrow St., Cambridge, MA 92138):

> The Chase Bank people have decided to run some of our ads, but not until June and then not at the extravagant $5 million they had discussed earlier, more like a million, which still isn't bad.

Henry Mead first meets his grandson, Adam Henry Agnello, 1978.

After my son was born, my husband and I moved from Oregon to Aitkin, in northern Minnesota, to publish my family-owned weekly newspaper. I didn't want to leave the Northwest but conceded, knowing we'd be closer to grandparents. Also, since my husband was going to be the breadwinner and I would stay home with our newborn, Adam, I believed his vote counted more about choosing a place to make a living. Once we were settled in Aitkin, I found myself alone during the day with a new baby, a newcomer to the community, with a husband who wasn't that happy himself. Then the sad saga of my brother's downfall began, and I was called to Boston to commit him to a psychiatric hospital.

Curt Mead, Adam and Evonne Agnello, Portland, Oregon.

THE COMMITTAL AFTERMATH

> Everything comes together and adds one knot more to the
> thread of life.
>
> —Pablo Neruda, *Births*

Two weeks after Dad and I committed Curt to Glenside Hospital, he was released and became homeless. Months later, he wrote my parents from Minneapolis:

> I'm not sure what my destiny is, but I believe I know where it is, and that's on the East Coast. That's where the mess is, and I can only clean it up if I'm there. I must face the people who know what happened to me, look them squarely in the eye, and show them I'm all right again.
>
> I've contacted an attorney to settle the business matters, and I've asked a friend to recommend an accountant to straighten out my taxes. I'm deeply appreciative of your love and assistance, but this mess is something I created and something I must handle on my own. My emotional pain has made me less extravagant and grandiose and more responsible and confident. I feel stronger and more energetic each day. Evonne has been very kind and supportive.
>
> I love you all very much,
> Curt

After a trip to Boston, Curt enrolled at the University of Minnesota to complete his degree and wrote:

> Dear Folks,
> School progresses all right. For the most part, reunions with my old friends have been disappointing for a couple of reasons: 1)

the dominance of alcohol in their lives—a great deal of their time is structured around drinking, often accompanied by TV, and 2) the lack of anything in their lives for which they apparently have any enthusiasm. Now, I don't expect most to have the intense passion I do for many things, but just a little enthusiasm would be nice, but I don't sense it. I could talk passionately, and at great length, about a host of subjects, from New York City to modern poetry, but I know my intensity sometimes intimidates people.

I still have periods of piercing loneliness and depression, but they're not as severe or as long as before. You asked what I would like for Christmas, so ... a book of Robert and John F. Kennedy's speeches. I don't know if there's a volume with both—if not, pick Robert Kennedy. I read and reread his biography, the one by Jack Newfield [RFK: A Memoir].

I'm sending my first submission to the *New York Times* tomorrow, a short piece they might run on their Op-Ed page. It's about the Vietnam vets I've met here whose lives ended the day they got out of the army and what a horrible thing our country did to them. It's passionate and, I hope, poignant. I love you very much. We're going to make it yet.

Curt

In December, my parents called me in Aitkin. Dad was agitated. "What's wrong?"

"Oh, Curt. The last couple of letters from him are full of wild ideas. He wants to start a Norwegian restaurant in Minneapolis and thinks, rather than spending Christmas in Seward, we should all go to Minneapolis to give cookies to Vietnam vets in the hospital. He wrote he didn't have time to make copies of the letters for you and asked me to read them to you."

"Sure. Go ahead."

Dear Family,
Since I've been here, I've asked about a hundred people, including some from the Sons of Norway, if there is a Norwegian restaurant in the Twin Cities and they all have said no. I believe so strongly about preserving our heritage and get upset when I see that history falling away. When one person said, "I think the Swedes have something somewhere," I responded, "Don't talk about Swedes to me. My cousin Ole fought the Nazis while the Swedes stayed neutral. I'm sure the Swedes are fine people, but

I'm proud that the Norwegians took a position on a great moral issue. I'm proud that they fought the Nazis, because the Nazis killed six million Jews, so don't tell me to go visit the Swedish Institute."

I mean well, of course, but people seem so surprised with my passion for a Norwegian restaurant. And because I love a good fight, I'm going to try to raise a little hell with a few folks to see if I can get someone excited about this. I'm going to volunteer my time to try to help somebody open a Norwegian restaurant, or better yet, a Norwegian village, in Minneapolis. It looks like an easy fight to me. People are always telling me I'm crazy, and maybe I am, but is it crazy to want a Norwegian restaurant in Minneapolis?

In another letter, he wrote:

To my family,

I have caused you all great pain this year, this worst and best year of my life. You have given me love, understanding, and tolerance, for which I am deeply grateful.

I have an idea for us this Christmas, something one American family could do which would make it memorable and might inspire others. What I propose is that Mother and Father and Evonne and her family come to Minneapolis a few days before Christmas and that mother direct us in baking as much as we can. While we're doing that, Father could teach us poetry, and we'd all have a good time. On Christmas Eve or Christmas Day, we'd have dinner at a nice restaurant so that mother wouldn't have to cook for once.

After that, we'd go to the Veteran's Hospital and hand out cookies to the patients, say Merry Christmas, and tell them that we appreciate the sacrifices they've made. Maybe if other people found out what we did, they would do the same. America has not taken good care of our veterans, and as you know, it makes me unhappy. It would be nice, and I think we'd remember for the rest of our lives the Christmas we went to the Veteran's Hospital to hand out cookies and say thanks. Let me know what you think.

Your crazy son and brother,
Curt

After Christmas, Curt wrote:

Well, I'm sorry you didn't see eye to eye with me about my idea for Christmas, so next week, I'm going to do some volunteer work myself at the VA Hospital. I was there tonight for a while, talking to some men, but mostly listening.

A few months later, Curt moved to New York City and wrote:

Well, I'm going to ask you to have a little more faith in me. I want you to be on my side. I'm trying hard to be a writer, writing every day and attending church nearly every day. I'm going to make it. This is the town for me. I'm lonely most of the time, but I'm in New York City, and I'm never unhappy when I'm in New York. I love you deeply. Have faith in me. Don't hassle my friends. Pray for me.

Love,
Curt

A few months later, he wrote to our father:

You write me one letter telling me you're convinced I need help, to which I respond, and then you pretend nothing happened. You decide to cut off my funding, which is your prerogative, of course, but the way you did it was punitive and coercive. I don't want to hear any more of this "come home" stuff.

Do you have any comprehension of the horror I've suffered the past fifteen months since that horrible two weeks I spent at Glenside where, by every measure of modern psychiatry I know, I was never crazy? Are you ever going to write me a letter and acknowledge this? And those people who told you I was crazy last year, are you ever going to tell me the truth about what you now see?

Is it beyond your ability to deal with this other than with the "put it behind you" flippancy you've given me the past year? Don't you know that remark is about the cruelest thing you can say to someone grieving?

I love you, but I'd love some honesty. If you can write me and say that I was crazy last year and deserved to be put in Glenside and have drugs forced on me, then you can forget I was ever your son because I will forget you were ever my parents. I want you to admit that you were wrong to commit me. If you can't admit that, then I don't care to ever hear from you again. I love you.

Curt

The next month, Curt sent a long, single-spaced letter to several friends. Here are excerpts:

Well, it's come to this. I'm writing the four of you, hoping one or all will help. I want to write a book on physics describing a new way of thinking about time, light, and matter. I believe it will rank in the history of science alongside Newton's Principia and Einstein's Relativity. I believe that the understanding I have will begin a new revolution in science. I hope someday it could be made public, but not for some time as it will allow the contemplation of a new generation of weaponry—new ways to protect our country from nuclear holocaust and preserve peace in the world.

I haven't spent a lifetime studying science; indeed, physics has been a serious concern of mine for only seven months. On the other hand, I have read scores of books and articles and would feel totally comfortable debating any physicist on this planet about quantum theory, relativity, the nature of the atom, and the nature of light. I have arrived at what appears to be a simpler explanation of nature than any theories I've read.

I believe I've discovered four principles that allow me to provide a unified explanation for all the phenomena of nature, from physics to chemistry, biology, geology, and astronomy. The four principals I have discovered, or will use, are: elasticity (amended from the way physicists currently understand it), bipolarity, tri-ontology, and quad cycylarity. My comprehension of nature allows me to consider new kinds of weapons. Specifically, it seems possible to create a weapon that could rupture missiles aimed at this country. It seems possible to imagine a way in which a bit of matter, perhaps a neutron, could be added to high frequency light, such as gamma rays, and for both to be shot into space at an oscillating pulse. I believe this might make it possible to shoot a neutron inside a missile, which could cause it to disintegrate.

I believe this book should be written and read as soon as possible. Besides this, I have come, in the past fifteen months, to new theories about theology, philosophy, psychiatry, aesthetics, history, government, politics, and economics. As you know, I have dedicated my life to the reduction of violence. I hope to continue the dream of Bobby Kennedy when he said that America could aspire to be the moral leader of the world. I want this planet never again to experience a Holocaust, Vietnam, or Hiroshima.

So, I'm appealing for your help. In the past fifteen months, my friends have deserted me, people have laughed at me, and only my family has supported me. But now, even they question my sanity and judgment. I have gone days without eating. I have slept with drunken bums in the Bowery. And although I hate ultimata, I must say that the lack of response will probably cause me to seek another country in which to work. So, please help. My bank account number is 445-739-182.

Sincerely,

Curt Mead

Later that summer, Curt wrote from New York:

My thinking about time, light, and matter is for the most part done, and now I must put it in writing. As you know from the letter I sent you, I would like to do it with meticulous scholarship, the kind I could be capable of doing with enough time. But no one here has any faith in me anymore. It's as though my past successes have all been taken away. I wish I could excuse you for your part in this. After all, you put me in that god-forsaken hospital. You've never said if you no longer believe that was the right thing to do. I can't believe you can now feel that that course of action was proper or moral.

A few months later, Curt wrote:

The radio and watch arrived—thanks for your continuing support. I'm going to see a navy admiral this week to talk about war and my ideas for its conduct at the end of this century. Further, because my comprehension of physics is so far ranging, I'm going to see if I can't make it have a practical application for the internal combustion engine. If I'm right about this, and I suspect I am, it will be a relatively simple matter to make engines much more powerful and efficient. Oh, the things I could do with a laboratory now—Faraday, Fermi, and Oppenheimer rolled into one. I sense that my long night of the soul is nearly over.

I love you, even though you make it difficult sometimes, you really do.

Curt

After that, Curt went underground and we heard nothing for more than a year. Dad filed a missing person report, but to no avail. It was especially hard at the holidays; he could have been dead and we wouldn't have known it. Dad kept repeating, as if to comfort himself, that he hoped Curt had his military dog tags, so if he was found dead somewhere, we'd be notified. Dad really knew how to look on the bright side.

I had a lot of balls in the air: dealing with my own distress about the loss of Curt, trying to cheer my parents (in their seventies), and trying to be a loving wife and mother. I had to be strong and pretended to cope. As the months wore on, my parents were increasingly distressed. In public, I kept a stiff upper lip and tried vainly to be a cheerleader of hope, but to no avail. I decided Curt was either dead or simply decided to excommunicate himself from his family. My father was an emotional wreck, and I wasn't much different. The stress took its toll on my marriage: I was depressed, my husband was unhappy, it was sixty below zero, and I was homesick for the Northwest. I began weekly psychotherapy and started recording my dreams, which were full of troubles and symbols I wanted to understand. I thought it might help get me out of depression. I'd never had so many dreams in such short a period. Here are fourteen I had during the last six months of 1980:

July 16: My watch is full of water. I try to run, but my legs won't move. I look in the mirror, and my face wobbles and changes. The small, quiet office where I meet my psychotherapist has been changed to a large auditorium. It's full of people, but no one notices me, so I reach out and touch someone. Curt is nearby but ignores me. I want to be noticed by him or anyone but feel lost in the crowd.

July 26: I'm running down dark creaky stairs, like those in the Aitkin newspaper office, to the bleak little room where Dad lived periodically.

July 27: I'm talking with Dad on the phone, but he can't hear me or won't listen.

July 28: I'm cooking, and the bottoms fall out of my pans. Why is this happening? I'm frustrated and screaming.

Aug. 8: Even though my parents were agile and healthy in their seventies, they arrived at the airport on crutches. It's clear their demise had been caused by Curt's errant behavior. I need to get wheelchairs for them but have great difficulty. Those in charge are all talking to each other on cell phones. I'm crying, breaking down, and then finally find some wheelchairs.

Aug. 10: I'm flying to our former home in Bend, Oregon, and the airplane crashes on takeoff.

Aug. 15: I'm leaping on a pogo stick. If I bounce too high, I lose control, and it's scary, but if I flutter my arms, I gain control and am relieved as I land safely.

Aug. 16: I get a call from Glenside where Curt returned asking for help, and they admitted him. I talk to him on the phone, and we discuss Thorazine and lithium, some of the drugs he took there.

Sept. 6: I'm at a banquet, see my shrink with his wife, and react by throwing a pie in her face.

Nov. 28: I jump off a dangerous cliff into water far below. As I try to escape, the rock wall to safety crumbles.

Dec. 1: I climb a rickety metal trellis trying to get home and am fearful of falling and not making it. Next, I'm on a steep, slippery stairway descending from the back of our house, terrified with fear.

Dec. 8: I'm in my junior high gym class dressing room, embarrassed about how I look. There are old women there with gray paint on their faces.

Dec. 12: I'm screaming at my mother for dishing up chocolate cake and sweets for me, and I angrily push the plates away.

Dec. 15: I'm cleaning a pair of old leather boots—black and heavily crusted with gunk—in the bathtub of the house where I grew up in Seward.

A month later, my husband asked for a divorce.

~ ~ ~

Two years later, I was thirty-five, divorced, and publishing our Aitkin paper when this letter arrived from Curt:

I have no money to send you a birthday present so I thought I'd write you a letter instead and devote some thought to you and our continuing dialogue. In many ways, I'm happy for you, because I sense you are experiencing the personal growth that often comes with divorce. You appear to be a bigger person than you were a few years ago. Your world is larger; you possess more self-confidence, even a bit more humor, and some wisdom. In many ways, you seem more relaxed about who you are and what you've done.

Think about your future, dream and raise your sights. Say to yourself, I can be bigger and happier than I am now. Learn to love yourself more, as well as things like ideals, art, and knowledge. Experience more. Think about going somewhere to let your dreams bubble to the surface. I want only the best for you, my sister. Happy Birthday. I love you. Best wishes for a happy and prosperous year.

Love,
Curt

The next month, he wrote a Christmas letter to our parents:

> I'd like to think that, all in all, it has been more a blessing than a curse to have me for a son, although I certainly acknowledge it has been both.
>
> The more I study humanity, the more I appreciate you two. In the past five years, especially, I have seen the sad results of mothers and fathers who did not have your relatively high standards of behavior. Consequently, I am grateful, especially to you, Father, whose long hours and selfless sacrifice did not go unnoticed, whose sobriety, reliability, honesty, and determination are qualities few sons see in their fathers.
>
> And, I am aware that the fruits of those long hours made it possible for me to be the untroubled free spirit I have been from time to time. No one is unhappier than I am that fame and fortune have been so elusive, but no one is more certain than I am that I will eventually capture those two maidens.
>
> Consequently, I am a happy man, confident of his future and not ashamed of his past. I'm grateful that you have been tolerant and understanding. We should be happy that we are all in good health once again. So, Merry Christmas, my parents. You are loved and appreciated by your sometimes eccentric son.

That spring, he wrote from Boston:

> Dear Folks,
>
> Success dangles before me, and I see doors that could open with celebrity and achievement. I spent Memorial Day alone in a city I once loved enough to think about being mayor—reminiscing and hoping. It's been five years since I was hospitalized and betrayed. My solace is that I have learned so much about life and science in the intervening years. I yearn to be among people again. I'm starting to answer ads in the paper for advertising and public relations work and suspect something will come of that. My writing continues to improve, so life looks better now than it has for some time, and I owe no small amount of gratitude to you for that.
>
> There seems to be such selfishness in the air here, an inability or unwillingness of people to give much of themselves to anything outside of themselves. I think many come here expecting a fairyland of wealth and happiness. When they don't find that, they retreat—sullen, cynical, and resigned. I hope I can find that not everyone is this unconnected.

With no work or money, Curt returned to Seward where he lived a reclusive life in the basement of our parents' home for the next several years. He had a painful muscular twitching, mostly in his jaw. He could control it when he was with people but usually when just the two of us were together, he would not. It was unpleasant to watch and made me feel horribly sad. We tried to get him to a doctor, but he refused. He was quiet, listless, and not a bit sociable. He slept most days and stayed up nights. He was angry and talked continuously about his bad experiences. I decided to share with Curt what I had written about his committal (which became the first chapter of this book), and he responded with a detailed and thoughtful reply.

> Dear Evonne,
>
> I am delighted to see that you are a pretty fair writer, but saddened to see the anguish of my experiences has colored your heart as it has mine. However, I must say that a disinterested reader of your story would conclude that I am nuttier than a fruitcake. All of the normal indices of paranoid psychoses are evident in your story: delusions of grandeur, ideas of reference, sense of persecution and omnipotence. You have captured a bit of the so-called truth of my life, and most important, your concern for me. I owe you a written response.
>
> I came to realize that, prior to the destruction of my life, I had been given gifts of people and experiences. I was groomed, challenged, and educated in ways I didn't entirely earn on my own. I came to see, for example, that the work I did for Ted Sorensen and the bank was more for my education than anything else. I realized that I had been given a great deal by the people who would betray me in 1979.
>
> Those people were all connected to what is sometimes called the Establishment, many of them with ties to the CIA. I've often wondered if they knew from the beginning that my fall from grace was a part of the plan. I remembered, for example, a short story Louise gave me for my birthday about a man who loses everything. I remembered her sadness and what she said to me shortly before my committal. I suspected she knew my fall was coming soon. In retrospect, I realized that my psychotherapy toughened me for what would follow.
>
> Conspiracy is almost impossible to prove, and I realized that for me to devote any effort to do so would be futile as I was,

at that point, an ex-mental patient. Then came my experiences on the streets and the warrior games at Fort Bragg, Quantico, Fort Hunter, Camp Pendleton, and San Francisco, where I came to believe that I was being prepared to lead. I met all kinds of people from throughout the world—Britain, France, Africa, and South America. Some were from the Mossad and other terrorist organizations; others were undercover agents and soldiers of fortune—a real rogue's gallery. It was a continuation of my soldierly education.

I'm still angry with myself for being gullible with those faceless, nameless people who manipulated me. I became aware that several agencies were interested in me because of my knowledge of physics and my emerging ideas on how weapons could be created. Then all the spies, spooks, and soldiers disappeared. So I went to New York City, where, lo and behold, a succession of people shows up who know a great deal about medicine and biology, to continue my education, I suppose. A few showed up in Boston last year—molecular biologists, chemists, and even a geneticist. I would be the eager student, pumping the experts for information in coffee shop and park bench conversations. These people would simply appear, answer my questions, give me lectures in a way, and then disappear. Others showed up almost regularly to give me a little money, pot, or shelter.

I'm so resentful of the manipulation that I've decided I won't become the American hero I thought I would. I'm angry at the arrogance of those who tried to make me into something they thought this country needed. I expect this letter will be read by others. I suspect you are still watched, your phone is tapped, and people in your life are more than they appear to be. I don't know this to be true, but I suspect it is. A woman I cared about died. It might have been a drug overdose, or it might have been murder. In one sense, I have forgiven my betrayers. I had to; my mental health required it.

I understand the psychiatric philosophy behind what happened to me, the unconscious and conscious manipulation. Certainly, I knew at the time of my incarceration that it was not a difficult act of subterfuge to get you and Father in on the joke, starting with phone calls to get you upset. My psychiatrist had learned enough about my family to know how to manipulate you. Certainly, in retrospect, some parts of it must look a bit ludicrous, even to you, being committed because I wanted to run for mayor of Boston and read a lot of books. Given my background and intellect, that was neither outrageous nor psychotic.

It was a cruel joke, and I'm still unhappy about how I allowed myself to be repeatedly tricked because I believed they would reward me. I used to dream of a party in which they all showed up to welcome me back into the fold. No one should be allowed to play with peoples' lives as they did with me. They may be doing it with others. The arrogance appalls me how they can do whatever they want and be accountable to no one.

I think it's best for all of us not to pursue this any further. I used to think about suing them, but the Establishment controls lawyers and judges and, barring someone's willingness to confess, it would be fruitless. I hope to write clever and funny things that people will enjoy and get enough money to leave the country ... my country, the one I used to love so passionately, the country I no longer love and the people I no longer care to serve. I think you should be circumspect in conversations about me with anybody. I suspect that I am not beyond further manipulation. Nor are you. Probably the safest thing for you is to continue to express publicly that your brother is hopelessly crazy.

I'm glad I studied physics and medicine. Maybe my betrayers and tormentors will confess and apologize for the abuse they heaped upon me. I hope you find something of value in this verbiage, and I'm sad my distress has become my family's distress. Best wishes, dear sister.

Love,
Curt

In the fall, Curt wrote again:

Dear Evonne,

Your birthday: a time to examine the past and consider the future. I sense I have very little credibility with you, so what I write may have little import, but I will try anyway.

First, let me reiterate that I care for you and I believe you and I have had honest dialogue through the years. But I sense that I confuse and trouble you. For the past several years, our discussions have left me with the impression that you feel trapped. However, you are not as trapped as most women your age. You have had more responsibilities, challenges, prestige, and freedom than most, and I know you know that.

I have repeatedly urged you to take a sabbatical of no less than three months, and I urge it upon you again. Take time to reflect on your life, to create new dreams and ambitions, to come to grips with who you are and what you want in the future. What is three months in a lifetime? I know you would never regret it, and I know it would be worthwhile and rejuvenating. You would grow from the experience, and I know you would be happy you did it. But it can't be a couple of weeks. It has to be three months or more. You must have time to let the past summarize itself and for new ideas to bubble up. They will—if you give your mind the proper environment.

   Love,
   Curt

BASEMENT TALKS

In every demented soul there is a misunderstood genius who frightens people and has never found an escape from the stranglings that life has prepared for him, except in delirium.

—Antonin Artaud, *The Man Suicided by Society*

It was Christmas Eve, 1984, and Curt and I were at our parents' home in Seward. They were in their late seventies and went to bed early, so Curt and I retreated to Dad's basement office, as we often did, to talk. It had been six years since Curt's committal to the psych ward, and we could have talked about anything, but Curt began the same awful tirade that he'd preached unrelentingly since his hospitalization.

"It was *so* wrong of you to send me to the loony bin," he said as he lit a reefer.

"Curt, you've told me this before. I know you feel this way. *Please*, can't we talk about something else?"

"You know why that jerk at Glenside couldn't look me in the eye and give me a straight answer about why I was being committed? You know why?" his pitch rising.

Oh, no...one of his manic blathering spells.

"It's because that guy at the hospital was part of the plot, too. Aren't you beginning to see, Evonne, how this all fits together?"

I shook my head, "No, I don't Curt. Please, let's talk about something else."

"You allowed yourselves to be manipulated."

"We were only doing what your doctor recommended."

"My dear sister, there are at least *five* sets of ears listening to the conversation we are having right now. Your life may be in danger. You should know that there are people watching you *all the time*. They are *paid* to do that. You should know that *all* your phone conversations are being tapped."

"Oh, Curt, I haven't done anything."

"Oh, Evonne," he said condescendingly, pacing the floor, puffing a cigarette.

I tried to enter the conversation, but he raised his voice, continued talking, and flashed his wild eyes to show he was not done.

"Haven't you heard of innocent victims? Read Robert Ludlum. If you knew what was best, we would go to California, Evonne. We need to take a long walk on the beach and talk. Remember the part in *The Godfather* where they turn up the music and TV and stand in the middle of the room to talk? We need to do that, Evonne."

"Let's talk about something else. How about Susan Sontag."

"Okay. That's actually a good idea. I was just reading her book, *Antonin Artaud, Selected Writings*." He goes to the bookshelf, pulls out a volume, thumbs through it, and continues.

"Susan writes a fascinating introduction—you should read this Evonne—talking about Artaud being locked up in the loony bin because of his spirited views, just like you and Pop did to me. Let's see, here it is, 'That's how society strangled all those it wanted to get rid of, or wanted to protect itself from, and put them in asylums.'

"Ah, yes, Artaud was imprisoned because he was crazy and wrote some of the most wrenching words ever put together. Artaud said a 'lunatic is a man who prefers to go mad … rather than forfeit a certain higher idea of human honor.'

"And then there's Delmore Schwartz. He used to say, 'Just because a man is paranoid doesn't mean his enemies aren't real.' Ah, Schwartz was a great man. He lived in New York City and was friends with Saul Bellow who raised funds for Delmore to get psychiatric care, but he refused the care and kept the money. Did you read *Humboldt's Gift*, Evonne?"

"No, I haven't."

"Well, you should. The title character was modeled after Delmore. Bellow won the Nobel Prize for that a few years ago, by the way. You really should read it."

"Well, Curt—"

"The truth of the matter, Evonne," he broke in again, "is that a woman *died* in my arms. I think it was the aristocrats, the spies, who did it, but there's no proof, of course. Her husband put a gun to his head, and then she became a lover of the big shots for money, but I was her friend, her lover, from whom she demanded no money."

"Curt, I want to believe that you're telling the truth, and it's my sisterly duty to hear you out. I'm sure there's some truth in what you say, but it's so bizarre. This hasn't been a conversation—it's been a ranting and raving monologue. Your ideas are full of delusions and paranoia."

If he's telling the truth, then he wouldn't be crazy ... and I don't want him to be crazy so I'll try to keep an open mind. Why would people in Boston want to frame Mud Boy? It's difficult to be around him when he paces, twitches, and grimaces as he's doing tonight. It sickens me to see his mind so horribly maimed.

"Why can't you put your life back together, Curt?"

"Oh, Evonne. Don't be so judgmental."

I tried to let go of thinking I could do anything to make my crazy brother sane. I longed for the brother I used to have, the playful one who listened and talked to me as a friend. But here he was, trying to pull me into his orbit of spies, microphones, and wiretaps. My heart ached as I tried to block his words as he paced the floor and continued ranting.

When he said, "Sometimes the radio plays music *just* to influence me," I'd had enough and rose wearily from my chair.

"I'm tired, Curt. I'm going to bed." I walked towards the stairs. A few steps up, I paused and gently added as lovingly as I could ... "Merry Christmas, Curt."

I thought, but did not speak, what Ophelia said in *Hamlet*, "What a noble mind is here o'erthrown."

A sane and healthy Curt *could* have been mayor of Boston, but not this one.

MOVING WEST

Happy families are all alike; every unhappy family is unhappy in its own way.

—Leo Tolstoy, *Anna Karenina*

After seven years in northern Minnesota, I moved far from my family. I found a great job in Tacoma, Washington, as assistant director of a non-profit association of daily newspapers in six western states. It was an expansion of my career and my life. I was now out of my father's shadow and physically distanced from Curt.

Always trying to understand my brother, I read about Delmore Schwartz. In Alfred Kazin's *Writing Was Everything*, I found words used to describe Schwartz that also described Curt. "[He] was drowning in a depression special to himself, hopelessly caught up in a tangled web of trying to prove that injustice, betrayal, was everywhere being directed to him ... He was a prisoner of his own superb intellectual training." I felt solace when I realized that many others had the illness that plagued my brother, but all the family scuttle took its toll on me.

That fall, he wrote:

> Dear Evonne,
> Euphoria is described as false elation, and I have sensed in your elation some euphoria. Every hello is also a goodbye. In your hopes and dreams of the future, do not forget to properly grieve the loss of Aitkin in your joy of moving to Tacoma. By looking back, one learns to look ahead with greater clarity, strength, and wisdom.

Grieving never really ends; your perspective just changes over time. For example, when I was hospitalized, I grieved the loss of my friends and business, but also the loss of what might have been—my being a candidate someday. You arrived in Tacoma, like every person who moves to a new place, full of hopes and dreams. However, be wary as they don't always come true and elation can turn to disillusionment.

I struggle to be a good and, perhaps, great writer. I struggle against loneliness, rejection, and the disappointment of unanswered letters. But it is joyous when I see my words behaving better than they used to, when my mind speaks with occasional power, passion, and eloquence. I struggle, too much it seems, but I keep focused on my goals and march on. You too, should set goals and keep marching on.

Finally, I recommend that you find an analyst to continue the work that can only go on in therapy. My analysis of your analysis was that you had come to the point of, what we used to call, the activation of the grandiose self. Grandiose is a term you once wrongly applied to my ambition to be an American Albert Camus. If I had said that I *was* an American Albert Camus, that would have been grandiose, but to *aspire* to be an American Camus is merely ambitious.

It was the activation of your grandiose self that allowed you to leave Aitkin. But your mind can still get better. With this change, you have the opportunity to grow, and continuing therapy would be so beneficial to you. Trust me on that. As someone who wants you to be happy, and as someone who believes he knows a great deal about psychiatry and psychoanalysis, please allow me to make the case for you to resume and finish the work you began with Dr. Willem Dieperink in Minnesota with a new doctor in Tacoma. The activation of the grandiose self creates a mélange of feelings from hostility to greater ego strength. With further therapy, you would be wiser, stronger, feel better about yourself, and be capable of more enthusiasm and enjoyment. I know this from experience. I hope you will do this. It is the smartest thing you could do right now. I'm happy and proud you made this move. It will be good for you. Most of all, best of luck. All of my hopes go with you.

The *Age* staff held a going away party for me in 1985 before I departed for Tacoma. I'm in the back row to the far left and next to me are Doris Kvanvig, Judy Peysar, Pat Bailey, Jack Wagner, Sharon Dotzler, Andy Skaj, and Daryl Hanson. In the front row are Sara Dotzler, Louise Lhotke, Terri Krause, Dawn Liljenquist, Ihlene Hejny, Carolyn Watson, and Gary North.

~ ~ ~

About a year later, Curt sent a letter for my son's ninth birthday:

Happy Birthday, dear Adam. Nine years old and ready to conquer the world or outer space or electricity or whatever your heart desires. Since I have no money to buy you a gift, I wrote you a little play. Dream dreams, little friend. Dream dreams and try to make them happen. But dream and dream and dream.

I love you dearly,

Your Crazy Uncle Curt

[Excerpts from] A one act play starring Adam Agnello, Curt Mead and Simone LaFleur.

Adam: So, look who's here, my crazy uncle Curt, late as usual. My birthday was yesterday, Uncle Curt.

Curt: Rub it in, Adam. Rub it in. By the way, I'd like to introduce Mistress Simone LaFleur from Paris. She's nine years old, too, and doesn't speak English, so I'll translate.

Adam: Why can't I have an uncle like everybody else? Instead, I get Curt. Lucky me, huh? Other kids have uncles who send them presents, and I get Curt and crazy letters. No one likes this play, Uncle Curt. It's boring. El stinko.

Curt: No truer words were ever spake. Simone said the same. As she was boarding the airplane to return to Paris, she said I was the stupidest playwright in the world and would never act in my plays again.

Adam:	I was thinking of telling you the same. What this play needs, Uncle Curt, is some dramatic tension, an interplay of good and evil, or something to sustain the audience's interest.
Curt:	From a nine-year-old boy-man, I have to hear this? Write your own play if you're so smart.
Adam:	I just may, Uncle Curt, and it won't be boring.
Curt:	Take a look now at the final scene. This is where we tug at the heartstrings of our audience.
Adam:	Right. Uncle Curt, there's no audience left. They're all out in the hall trying to get their money back.
Curt:	Maybe someday I can teach you a little about playing pool and judo.
Adam:	Promises, promises, Uncle Curt.

Haunted by Curt's words to seek a psychiatrist, in December 1986, following a romantic breakup, I knew I was depressed enough to need professional help. The euphoria of the move west was magnificent, but it didn't last. I decided that life was not meant to be this glum for this long, so I turned to the Yellow Pages and found hundreds of psychiatrists. I decided to trust my intuition and as I read the names, circled those that resonated. I also considered location—no need to drive far with so

Adam and Evonne Agnello, 1987.

many choices. *Ah, here's one just a few blocks from my office*, and I liked his name, Randolph Peterson.

After several sessions, I wrote in my journal:

I'm seven weeks into therapy and still crying every Monday. Yet, there is a gradual feeling of relief. Seeing mother sad and depressed and thinking I was responsible. I had a dream that I was in the back shop of our Seward newspaper, by the grungy old toilet room, trying to escape and finally getting out the back door. Consciously, I know I'm okay—now to get the unconscious to know that.

Shortly after I moved to Tacoma, Curt moved to San Francisco and wrote:

I began my telephone fundraising for the theatre last night and was the champ of the evening. I feel satisfied with my progress. I'm sending off more letters today—finding a variety of writing and public relations work available.

When I talked with him, I could tell he felt happy, clever, and smug doing work he valued while his bizarre and awkward facial tic was invisible. Curt sent me a copy of a letter he'd sent to an executive at the United Nations, Ann Garrels.

Dear Ms. Garrels,

As a struggling poet and playwright, I often select, from the cosmos of women who don't give a damn about me, a name to ponder. Writing to a woman who has never heard of me is a warm-up exercise I do before my serious writing. And today, you are that lucky woman. You were this classy mell doing the early reading at NBC, and now you're over at the UN.

In a play that someday may get rave reviews in Gotham (the one I am writing), there is a female TV journalist. She is a sympathetic figure and holds up well against the savage verbal abuse heaped upon her. She has moments of poignancy and existential puzzlement, as the archivist must. Standing witness to a planet gone mad with self-destruction is a curious position indeed. Recording this insanity daily, presenting it with a straight face to the world, showing the drama of man's folly, cruelty, and ignorance is the road of the writer.

Not bad, huh? A little overdone perhaps, but I say, let the woman have her moment of insight. Not every TV journalist is a brash and shallow, pretty-faced pea brain. Take you—I have the impression that you are a woman of depth and urbanity, perhaps even literacy. Best wishes to you, Ms. Garrels.

Curt Mead

In a letter to our parents, he wrote:

> My health is excellent, both physical and mental. I plan to begin writing about medicine, a field I have studied diligently the past six years and in which I think I have a thing or two to say. Soon, however, I may be a somewhat famous playwright earning royalties … but that's not going to happen before Christmas. I have no doubt, however, that it *will* happen.
>
> It's been a year of change for the family. Evonne and Adam to Tacoma and Curt to San Francisco. Count our blessings. We all have our health. Death has not intruded upon us. None of us is broke or deprived. I know I will soon be a great writer. Unlike most families on the planet, we have been blessed with material wealth and conviviality. We all talk with each other amicably, which is rare in families. We don't face the sad ravages of poverty or disease.

In another letter:

> I've had three good days at my typewriter and sent some pieces to the *San Francisco Chronicle* and *The New Yorker*.
>
> Camus died twenty-six years ago today [January 4, 1960] on a lonely country road in France, the victim of a car accident. He would be impressed to know how he touched the life of a small-town boy from Nebraska. He would be pleased to know that an awkward country kid read his words most of his adult life and thought long and hard about what he was trying to say. He would be pleased to know that this country journalist aspired to be known as an American Albert Camus.
>
> I've secured a lucrative part-time job raising money for the San Francisco Symphony. It begins tomorrow and means I will have income to cover my expenses and then some. I sense this will be a good year for me. I'm happy about my new job and the progress in my writing. I hope all is well with you.

In another letter:

> I worked hard at the theatre this week—again the eager beaver, just like the old days, always doing more than necessary. Richard Nixon and Mario Cuomo speak at ANPA [American Newspaper Publishers Association] holding its convention here, and I may try to attend. I have fond memories of Cuomo. He and I spent a lot of time together in 1977, just Mario and Curt, discussing the world. Cuomo was on the cover of *Time* this week and made me

remember how charming and shrewd he could be, how he had to challenge and spar verbally all the time, how he never let down his guard. That's the Jean Paul Sartre in me. The Camus says hold back, stay disengaged, and remain the observer.

I had my first week with two new part-time jobs. This afternoon, I called people on the phone peddling Time-Life books. So many snarled at me, snorted how they don't read books anymore. I muddled through, but it bothered me that they don't read books—and even more so that they bragged about it. In the evenings, I call for the theatre. Here I speak to gracious people who appreciate my wit and style. It's a treat to speak to so many charming women, as I did this week, calling previous donors. I'm coming to like San Francisco again. Every day I see people from all over the world. It's a city that often pleases the eye with its architecture and many lovely streets—a walker's delight. The women look strong and intelligent.

In a later letter:

The telephone solicitation business can be brutal. I think I'd have better luck calling members of the B'nai B'rith asking for money for Nazis. The disconcerting necessity of mine to pump my jaw, my affliction as I call it, got worse before it got better. There were times when I had no choice but to sit and endure the painful experience for hours at a time. They don't notice it at work as I sit in a cubicle. I've had moments and sometimes hours, when I sensed profound contentment, when the nobility of my intellectual aspirations seemed to have its own rewards. I remember doing this before, turning pain into strength, anguish into confidence. I remember the good years in Boston, in 1977 and 1978—the year people told me I should run for office myself. I think I'll do some writing on liberty tonight. I have devoted great study and contemplation to the idea of extending the blessings of liberty. Thanks for everything.

Love,
Curt

In another letter:

I hope nothing in my last note upset you. I didn't mention it at the time, except to call it my affliction, but it was my sole daily activity for four months. For ten, twelve, sometimes eighteen hours a day, I sat in a chair, moved my jaw up and down and experienced exhausting pain. It was something I had to tough out, part of the price I had to pay for whatever wisdom I may offer the world. What I experienced might be called the stress of the truth seeker, the struggle of the mind and body to distill, clarify, and conquer. What made it worthwhile was what I've learned about the biology of the mind and body and the electrochemical processes of consciousness itself, insights I might be able to profitably share with psychiatrists. Enough of that.

My love and gratitude,

Curt

Later that summer, he wrote to me:

I expect to fly to Tacoma to visit you when the folks are there next month. I look forward to cordial conversations and hope we can avoid the unpleasantness that has, sadly, too often colored our time together. I believe you're displaying a healthier attitude than most women your age when it comes to mothering. What parents do to their children is not always a pretty picture.

My life remains simple, monastic, arduous, and satisfying. I think of these past years as Gandhi called his time in the wilderness, his satyagraha, his quest. Sitting in my room, working hard in my mind, I am consoled by the knowledge that others I have loved, Camus, Sartre, Einstein, and Gandhi, have all paid the dues I'm paying. The physiological component of the search for new comprehension is surprising. This is the kind of writing that upsets the parents so.

Following Curt's visit to Tacoma, he wrote:

Our time together was marked by tension and hostility, as has often been the case these past years. It's sad that I upset you, as I have before, with my passion and animated style. Ultimately, if you want to feel better and grow wiser, you must continue your therapy and dig out the sadness until it is gone and then you will be happier. Please, Evonne, continue with a psychoanalyst.

I'm happy about my decision to move to Paris. I wish I would have accomplished better writing here, but I see the issues of medicine with greater clarity now. It sounds as if you're a little in love, which is what you wanted to be, so I'm sure you're a bit happier.

Love,

Curt

Curt wrote to Mother:

> This letter is a demonstration of my affection for you. This is
> your son, the doctor, giving his mother free medical advice. I am
> happy that you have decided to stop taking Persantine. I think
> you should go to Dr. Hoff and tell him that you would like to try
> Valium, a drug recommended by your son, a (self-proclaimed)
> psychoanalyst. I would suggest a very mild dose, fifteen to thirty
> milligrams a day, in five or ten milligram pills, taken three times
> a day. I'd like you to take Valium for two weeks and see if you
> don't feel less anxious, less restive, and more energetic. If you
> notice none of these effects, then quit taking the pills.
>
> Love,
> Curt

That summer, I heard a grand symphony perform Holst's The
Planets, saw a wonderfully funny play, *Angry Housewives*, and hiked
the Lake Quinault and Hoh River trails in the Olympic National Park.
I read John Updike's *The Witches of Eastwick* and Sam Shepard's play,
A Lie of the Mind, where human weaknesses are laid bare, revealing
life's imperfections. I camped at La Wis Wis campground, near the base
of Mount Rainier. I had a dream of a big pot of dangerously boiling
water; I put on a lid, and then everything was okay. Later, I was in a
dark, deep cavern and climbed down some steps—remindful of the
basement stairs in our Aitkin newspaper.

Curt wrote:

> I continue my struggle between the self who writes and the
> self who does not, the self who doesn't want to linger in the past
> and the one who does. It's my new self being created, and it's
> a wondrous experience. Sometimes there are moments when
> I feel deep contentment and have glimpses of great clarity in
> what I've studied.

The next year, 1991, Curt wrote:

> Dear Evonne,
> First of all, congratulations on the excellent showing in your
> media law class and your assumption of more duties at work.
> These both sound encouraging, and I'm happy for you. I wrote
> to the parents saying I finally agreed with them that I should
> return to Nebraska to have my teeth implants and continue my

writing. My affliction continues in my jaw and all over my body but shows a little improvement. Best wishes to you.
Love,
Curt

When Curt came to Seward for his dental work—he had neglected his teeth for years—he found a way to earn money at a medical laboratory in Lincoln. The business provided fees for people who would take experimental prescription drugs and allow themselves to be monitored. Curt did this periodically for months to earn money. Usually, he would take medicine and then report for tests, but because the pay was much higher, sometimes he agreed to be confined for a few days.

In the fall of 1989, he wrote from the Lincoln lab:

Dear Evonne,
I'm happy to report that I've decided to move to Boston in a few weeks. I remember arriving there six years ago with eight dollars and the clothes on my back, hoping that someone would have pity and take me in. That didn't happen, and I spent the next eight months on the streets.
Boston was kind to me for many years, and I have a host of treasured memories there, of former Mayor Kevin White, with whom I spent such a fascinating time in 1975, teaching my Harvard class that year, and the fine men and women who seemed to like me. Oh God, how I dread this final week here. It reminds me of my Glenside confinement, and that's always unpleasant. But it's money, and money buys me escape.

A few weeks later, he wrote from Boston:

I'm glad I came here. My writing improves. My affliction continues, but I remain optimistic. I expect I'll be taking some stupid telephone job to keep food in my belly and a roof over my head.
Love,
Curt

A few months later, he wrote:

Well, I've been remiss in responding to your kind letter of last month. It's been rough for me—dealing with my affliction is demanding. When I'm with people, I can control the twitching, and they have no hint of the pain I'm in, since I don't grunt and groan as I do when I'm alone. When I'm able to think and write, I work on my play. I think it's going to be powerful and poignant.

I ran an ad in the personals that read, "Cinderella Complex no longer welcome. Journalist now seeks Jeanne d'Arc Complex, Madame Currie Complex, Isadora Duncan Complex, Hannah Arendt Complex, 30–45, the crazier the better." I received fifteen replies, of whom I've met five, one a psychiatrist, a lovely woman from Texas, another a psychiatric social worker, an intelligent but portly woman, and one is an archaeologist who works at Harvard. I wanted intelligent women and I got them. I'm selective in telling my history. I believe I'm moving towards something profound and significant.

I wish I could tell you that my affliction is better, but it is not. I've told nothing of this to the parents, to spare them concern. It's good that you're continuing psychotherapy and dealing with childhood resentments. I got to play with cameras and printing equipment, and you learned how to be a mommy. The expectations were different for us. Feminism had not yet happened. You sound healthier than you've ever been. At the theatre company, I am a star fundraiser once again, but how much more I want to be a star playwright. My best to you.

Love,
Curt

For my son's twelfth birthday, Curt wrote:

My Dear Nephew Adam,

I've sent you two books. One is a good and simple story called *The Pearl*, written by an author of many fine books, John Steinbeck. I hope you enjoy it. The other is *Johnny Tremain*, a hero of the American Revolutionary War. As you read it, you can think about Boston and New England, which is where I am living now and where you might come and visit me someday. I'd like that.

I've also sent you a magazine I used to like a great deal when I was your age, *Mad Magazine.* And, I've sent you a book about Harvard College. In a few years, you'll be thinking about college, and you might want to think about an Ivy League school. You might not. There's plenty of time for us to talk about college. I've always liked Harvard because they paid me to teach there years ago.

A U.S. Senator called me this morning, an old friend of mine named John Kerry. I may be doing some writing for him. I had written him a letter that he liked.

I love you as a son, dear Adam. I want you to be happy, read books, think for yourself, and stay single. These are my hopes for you, to pursue your dreams, happily and determinedly. I will always urge you to dream and to pursue your dreams.

I love you dearly,

Curt

In the fall, Curt wrote Adam again:

Thanks so much for the Gary Larson calendar. Your uncle is lucky to have a nephew like you. I've enclosed some information about where I work, a shelter for soldiers living on the streets. I'm helping them raise money and feel good about that. I'm being more public than I have for some time and that's good.

Also, I've enclosed a story I've written about my experiences on the streets, "Sidewalk Lamentations," about standing witness to the victims. Actually, Adam, I'm proud of the man who submitted himself to the life in the streets that I write about. At the time, your mother and grandparents didn't understand what I was doing, but I always knew that my experiences would make a good story someday and be good preparation for a renewed political life.

And, as I always say, Adam, pal of mine, read books and think for yourself. Your uncle is making progress as a consultant and writer. A few more revisions and I might have something a magazine would print. I so much want to be a published writer.

Sidewalk Lamentations

Stand Witness to the Victims

This was written by Curt, eleven years after his homeless period, at age forty-four.

On the streets, it is said that God created the homeless so that welfare mothers would have wretches they could look down upon. On the streets, God is alive. In the mission, at the obligatory service before dinner, the homeless strain to believe. With all their might, they yearn for the God who has deserted them. Around the trash can fires at night, they talk of the Guy upstairs who will look out for them. Living in hell, they know that there is a heaven waiting for them.

There is comfort in eating food from garbage cans. One is eating better than most of the children in the world. There is more nutrition in America's discarded refuse than in the meals of most children. For me, it was better to eat food from garbage cans than to accept charity dinners. Standing in lines next to puffy-eyed men with slouching shuffles was too much to bear. The volunteers who serve the meals brace valiantly to smile, but the tragedy shows in their eyes. Were there really so many broken people? In the richest nation on earth, how could there possibly be so many suffering like this? It was better for *me* to avoid these stark statements and instead rummage through garbage cans for dinner.

You must stand witness to the victims and the oppressed—that's what Albert Camus said. So, I spent two years on the sidewalks of urban America, living a desolate, barren, and homeless life. It was an act of oblation, a submission of the self to horrors, to experience squalor and violence and to know how the poorest Americans live. It was an act of atonement and expiation for the failures of politics.

To follow in the footsteps of Mahatma Gandhi, to assume the horror as one's personal responsibility, to be a philosopher-penitent, a Buddhist monk, a samurai in training, a soldier. There is no kindness on the streets, no dignity. The homeless hitchhiker becomes an easy target for the hostility in America. People scowl as they pass by, pretend to stop, and then speed away. They throw things at you. They aim their cars at you and make you jump to safety. Alone and vulnerable, one becomes the focus of free-floating rage.

On the sidewalks, you are invisible to your fellow citizens but not to the thugs who beat you up. To be sober, in my thirties and in good shape spared me the worst. Yet, on several occasions, I was beaten, punched, and kicked—even stabbed once. After these episodes, I found myself lying in alleys, a quivering bundle of pain and anguish, a pulsating puddle of a man. But I realized that I had it better than most on the streets. The elderly drunken men had it worse, and the women had it the worst. Repeatedly raped and beaten, some women on the streets simply fade away into insanity. I was witness to collapses of the self, minds in so much pain they simply retreated to places where no one could reach them. I watched people deteriorate into nothingness, frightened and skittish, eyes full of fear and desperation.

What sort of a nation would allow such horrors? My contempt grew for a country that did nothing while millions suffered unspeakable crimes and neglect on the streets. At night, I would yell at President Reagan. I would yell at Congress. I would yell at America.

Stripped down to nothing but the clothes on my back, without a penny to my name, I was in a world where no one smiles and there is no dialogue. You learn who you are when everything is taken away. It was an exploration of the self, one's history, ideals, and patriotism. I had something most homeless people never had—memories of women who had loved me. I would imagine them with me and would talk to them as I shuffled along the streets. To all appearances, I was just one more ambulatory schizophrenic, talking to people who weren't there. At night,

I would imagine them holding me, and I'd sob convulsive and cleansing tears for my suffering and the suffering all around me.

There are so many veterans on the streets of America whose life in the service of their country weakened them. Disillusioned by their wartime experiences, they came home to a country they didn't understand and which offered little compassion. They were in bad shape before they were soldiers, and their patriotic sacrifice damaged them even more. Bitter and betrayed, they sought solace in booze and drugs.

I called out to some of the honorable men I had known in politics to join my soldiers' council. They would be my wartime buddies on the battlefield of the sidewalks. They were my imaginary medics among the battered and betrayed. I would yell, "Medic!" but there were no medics to come to the aid of the suffering.

A line from T. S. Eliot's *The Love Song of J. Alfred Prufock* repeated in my mind, "I should have been a pair of ragged claws scuttling across the floors of silent seas." What evil was this, which did nothing in the face of such obvious suffering? What treason was being perpetrated by the president and Congress? Traitors. What else could they be called, to ignore such an obvious festering sore on the body politic?

I talked for hours to Mahatma Gandhi and blamed him for my decision to crucify myself upon the streets. Gandhi promised a reward for self-induced suffering in the pursuit of wisdom and truth. For ten years, I could not write of the experience. What reward was that, Mahatma? There was only enormous sadness. A small-town boy from Nebraska, I was a patriot who lost his country somewhere out there on the sidewalks. I had worked in politics and been a political consultant. I had worked for Boston Mayor Kevin White and JFK counselor Ted Sorensen. I had worked for senators, congressmen, governors, and attorneys general. I had been a speechwriter. I had believed in politics. But the disease of the national mind was deeper than any political remedy could hope to address—brutality and banality everywhere.

The sickness was personified by a president who stole tough-guy lines from the movies and postured for the cameras. What did he know of life on the streets? What did the self-righteous moral mutants know of the battered children who grow up to be battered adults? How could America reward such petty minds with such apparent affection and approval? Who should one find more disgusting, the leaders who said and did nothing, or the populace who seemingly loved them so? Who were more contemptible, the moral cowards who pretended to be leaders, or the people who elected them?

What surgery was needed? Where did one begin to exorcise the evil? What medicine could assault such an overwhelming illness? What was there to do?

Stand witness to the victims, Camus said.

I'm trying Albert, I'm trying.

~ ~ ~

In the meantime, I had a flurry of dreams again. I found my bond to Aitkin was stronger and stayed longer than I expected. For years after leaving, I had recurring and distressing dreams about living there. Several involved the dark stairway in the newspaper shop that led to the basement where the staff break room had been transformed into a spooky dungeon. Other dreams involved challenging situations that I remarkably and unusually resolved. Another time, I was in something like a coalmine—it was dark, damp, and scary. I returned many times to creepy, creaky, and shadowed stairs leading downward. I would awake with deep sadness and darkness. One time, I was in my car trying to leave town, but the roads were flooded. There were emergency barricades at each exit, and the police said it was impossible to leave.

Weeks later, I dreamed I was stranded in the print shop of the Aitkin newspaper and couldn't leave. I awoke frightened. The next week, I had another dream about going to the Aitkin newspaper office, but there was no desk for me. It was dark and boring, and I wanted to leave. Why did I keep having these dreams? It'd been six years since I'd left.

A POLITICAL PRISONER
IN GERMANY

I n 1993, Curt was in Boston, and I was in my eighth year in Tacoma. Mom had been in the nursing home about a year, and Dad was living at home, a few blocks away. Curt and I would often meet in Nebraska, especially around the holidays.

During one such visit, I asked Curt, "So, what happened in Germany last year that got you so upset?"

"Well, Evonne, I had some pretty amazing experiences there. I wrote a story about them and sent it to Steve Mindich. I think I mentioned him to you some years ago when he and I traveled in the same circles when I was a political consultant."

"No, I don't remember."

"That was when I was lucky enough to be outbid by Ralph Fine and Marty Linsky to buy the *Real Paper* in 1975. I've sure been all over since then."

"Ya. I—"

"Now, this is important, Evonne. I want you to listen carefully because all the events I'm about to tell you are true, and I have documents to prove some of them. So, here's the deal—I was arrested at the airport as I tried to leave Frankfurt. The charge was credit card fraud, even though I had used my own valid credit card and the credit card company had accepted the charge."

"How could they do that?"

"Well, it was a phony charge. They knew it, and I knew it."

"Why had they arrested you?"

"It could have been something I said or wrote when I was in Germany. Or maybe it had something to do with the Kurdish terrorist attacks on Turkish Embassies. Did it have something to do with, what I assume is, my long Interpol file as an associate of unsavory characters from around the world? Perhaps my sneering commentary on German aristocrats had offended the powerful men."

"Well, Curt, your words certainly can be caustic at times, something you inherited from our father, I think."

"I *wanted* to offend them. They might have pulled a few strings to punish me for my American impudence. Who knows? I was held for twenty-eight days and not allowed phone calls or legal counsel. I know that letters I wrote were never delivered. I know that, if not for the diligent help from Ms. Cathy Carrier of ATT Universal MasterCard, they might have held me longer. I gave them a good show when I was in the Hanau Detention Center. I was the American prisoner they loved to pick on, because I would pick back at them.

"In jail, there were some sixty desperadoes from around the world, known associates of demimonde fugitives and charlatans. Also in the mix were spies, counter spies, terrorists, and counter-terrorists. I met Oriental thugs, Yakuza, and all sorts of unsavory characters from North Korea, Nepal, Thailand, and Vietnam. They had all been in the same lowlife watering holes I had been in, gathering gossip. Perhaps some of the Axis power reunion stories I had been hearing were true. Perhaps my innocent jokes about Axis power revenge in the presence of bankers from Japan, Italy, and Germany hit a raw nerve. And yet in the seedy dives of Sexstrasse (the red light district of Frankfurt), I could see Sergei, Gustav, Zuzu, and Mahmoud from Iraq, Daud from Iran, Latif from Syria, Ali from Libya, Muffie from Morocco, Alfie from Algergia, and Omar from Egypt."

"Oh my, Curt. What a wild story. Do you think—"

"Wait, get this. What on earth was Giap duc Tet, my old friend from Paris of years ago, the Viet Cong guerrilla theorist, doing in Frankfurt and staying at the Steigenberger Frankfurter Hof Hotel just as I was?

It's a high-class place, and thugs like us are usually not welcome. Here, I'll read from my letter to Mindich:

> "Giap," I squealed in delight and terror when I saw him in the salon the day after Chuck Berry left. "Giap duc Tet, what is a god-dammed commie, so-called friend of the working class, doing, staying in the finest hotel in Frankfurt? Finally sell out?"
>
> Giap was silent but an inscrutable smile crossed his taciturn Vietnamese face. In 1986, Giap and I had spent many drunken hours in Paris healing our Vietnam wounds with burgundy, tears, and yelling. It had been cathartic for both of us and for the French Foreign Legionnaires who listened and watched our *recherché du temps perdu* Vietnam.
>
> But that was seven years ago. Lots of water had flowed under our bridges since, and it had brought us a bit of the good life, as I could clearly see from Giap's dapper Italian clothes and unusually clean fingernails; and the same was true for me. We were enjoying the good life at the Frankfurter Hof, and the German bankers were paying for both of us, I discovered much to my horror in our drunken reunion.
>
> "The German Bankers have brought you to Frankfurt? They're paying for my expenses, too. What on earth are they up to, Giap?"
>
> It was at that moment that one of the strangest couples I have ever seen joined Giap and me at our corner table. Giap rose instantly to greet them as long-lost friends.
>
> "Good evening. I'd like to introduce Mad Ludwig, the Baron Spritzen-Sie Von Stumpfen and his Consort, Francesca Borgia, the Corsican Contessa."
>
> I knew instantly this was going to be a strange night. The Baron and the Contessa had clearly seen better days. She was in her late thirties and reminded me of the kind of woman one might get breeding Goldie Hawn (at her wackiest) with Attila the Hun. There was intensity to the woman, heightened only by the old and tattered nature to her once elegant gown. Stranger yet was her opening comment to me, as she fell gracefully to her divan. Solemnly, slowly, she announced that for the evening she was not the Corsican Contessa, but tonight she was Bouncing Betty from Bethlehem.
>
> The Baron, on the other hand, was a paragon of sanity as he removed his monocle and dropped it into Giap's brandy snifter. He pulled it out by its strap, licked it gently, and then wiped it with a small chamois cloth he had tucked in his cummerbund, part of his

shopworn black tuxedo. I felt I had fallen into *Ninotchka,* the 1939 film with Greta Garbo. Mad Ludwig launched immediately into a long rumination on Immanuel Kant's unheralded contribution to American rock and roll music. Chuck Berry had been staying at the Frankfurter Hof, and he and the Baron had apparently spent a night or two discussing Aristotelian and Kantian contributions to down-home blues.

"Whew. That's an incredible tale, Curt. I'm tired and am going to bed." That fall, Curt wrote me from Boston:

> I'm enclosing a couple of Pop's recent letters. He's quite distressed and mean spirited, and I'm unable to say or do anything to lesson his anguish. It's the ugly side of fathers and sons. He beats me up emotionally when he senses I'm weak and vulnerable. He's done it many times in the past, and I've seen him do it to many people. It's an ugly side of him, and I fear it will only get worse as he gets older. I hope you can have a calming effect on him. It's as if he has resentful bile simmering inside and every now and then needs to let it out.
> Better days ahead,
> Curt

Dad was eighty-five, living at home, had prostate cancer, and was getting weaker. He'd been in and out of the nursing home where Mom had lived the past two years. His doctor said he had low iron, so he asked me what he should eat to build his blood.

"Spinach, Dad. Eat a lot of spinach and a tablespoon of blackstrap molasses every day. You can get twenty percent of your daily requirement of iron in that one dose of molasses."

Christmas was stressful in Nebraska—trying to talk Dad out of depression, being cheerful with Mom in the nursing home. My work was full of challenges and satisfaction. With our new computers and modem, I had an exciting road ahead. But, I needed a breather and decided to spend a few days in the Olympic Rainforest, just a couple hours from my home. I wanted the exhilaration of hiking in the quiet woods. I needed to step away from work, the responsibilities, mail, phones, and demands. How proud I was to realize I needed this self-nurturing. How full of energy and vitality I'd be when I'd return. I'd leap joyfully into the challenges with memories of this quiet time to read, write, think, and hike.

~ ~ ~

I find no greater peace, no greater joy than experiencing natural beauty, hearing the roar of the canyon waterfalls, seeing the pure white light in the water crashing over rocks, surrounded by lush green moss, lichen, and towering trees with delicate greenery gently swaying in the breeze. I felt happy because that was where I needed to be. The peace, clarity, and soul rejuvenation that come from the rainforest are profound. A man named Sven had written in the guesthouse journal were I stayed this lovely thought, "As I moved through the forest, it moved through me." The land has the highest concentration of organic material found in any ecosystem in the world, and this density tunes my senses to a sharper level. My soul absorbed life there as the forests do the mist, weaving a rejuvenating spell. A sign on the forest path asked me to consider how I fit into the web of life. And I did. I believe that magical and spiritual things happen because of that high-density biomass.

Becoming emotionally strong by these experiences turned out to be only partly satisfactory against what I'd face next.

PART II

THE EVENTS

1994 - 2000

WHAMMY

When I was young I believed death to be a phenomenon of the body; now I know it to be merely a function of … the minds of the ones who suffer bereavement.

—William Faulkner, *As I Lay Dying*

It was early afternoon on a sunny July day, and I had settled into a chair on my deck to read a stack of newspaper trade journals—a staple of my job—when my phone rang.

"Hello."

"Hi, Evonne. This is Clark Kolterman."

"Hi, Clark."

"I've got some bad news. Your father died. He didn't show up for coffee this morning, so we went over to the house. We saw him through the garage windows slumped over in his car. When we broke in the back door, we could smell carbon monoxide. It was suicide."

While I was riveted, it was not a complete surprise because Dad had talked about this more than once.

I flew to Nebraska, Curt flew in from Boston, and Adam from New Hampshire. Curt immediately stepped up to the plate and said he would write a eulogy.

At the house, I found four large cans of spinach and blackstrap molasses in Dad's cupboard. He was intent on building his body and fighting the inevitable—for a while. Here was a man who began penniless and fatherless and, with decades of hard work, owned two weekly newspapers. His aim was always clear—he wanted his kids to have a good education and a better life (meaning more financial security) than he and my mother had.

In his later years, he said, "I have been in the newspaper business all my life, and any accumulations in my balance sheets have not been due to big decisions or even smart ones. Rather, they may be credited to forty years of seventy-hour work weeks."

He railed about the cost of nursing home care and was concerned that his family urgently needed his money. Mom's nursing home costs continued to escalate, Curt had no means of support, and my son would be headed for college in a few years.

At the mortuary visitation, I heard the voice of a little girl and turned to see a young woman, obviously her mother, and unknown to me, toting a teary-eyed young child.

"Hello," I said. "I'm Henry's daughter."

"Hello. It's nice to meet you. I'm Jill Norris. I got to know your father when he'd come to visit your mom in the nursing home. I'm a nurse there."

"Well, thank you. Thank you for coming."

"And this is my daughter, Cady."

The little one turned her face around from being buried in her mother's neck, her eyes red from crying and cheeks dripping with tears.

"Cady wanted to come and say goodbye. Your father used to recite the *Moo Cow Moo* to her."

"Oh, my. Oh yes—I know that poem well. Dad recited it to me, too."

"As soon as your dad would recite the poem, Cady would beg him to say it again and again … and he would. I heard him give a program at Kiwanis where he recited so many poems from memory."

"Yes, he and my mom were both big poetry fans. They told me that during their courtship, they used to read poems to each other."

"It was amazing how many he had memorized."

"He used to say he had about a hundred and twenty-five he knew by memory."

"He was such a dear man."

"Thank you so much for coming. Bye bye, Cady."

After they left, my eyes filled with tears, and I sat down and sobbed. Here's the poem , beloved by children, written by Edmund Vance Cooke.

The Moo Cow Moo

My papa held me up to the Moo Cow Moo
So close I could almost touch,
And I fed him a couple of times or so,
And I wasn't a 'fraidy cat, much.

But if my papa goes in the house,
And my mamma she goes in too,
I keep still like a little mouse
For the Moo Cow Moo might Moo.

The Moo Cow's tail is a piece of rope
All ravelled out where it grows;
And it's just like feeling a piece of soap
All over the Moo Cow's nose.

And the Moo Cow Moo has lots of fun
Just switching his tail about,
But if he opens his mouth, why then I run,
For that's where the Moo comes out.

The Moo Cow Moo has deers on his head,
And his eyes stick out of their place,
And the nose of the Moo Cow Moo is spread
All over the Moo Cow's face.

And his feet are nothing but fingernails,
And his mama don't keep them cut,
And he gives folks milk in water pails,
When he don't keep his handles shut.

But if you or I pull his handles, why
The Moo Cow Moo says it hurts,
But the hired man sits down close by
And squirts, and squirts, and squirts.

Here's part of Curt's eulogy:

Henry Mead lived an exemplary life, devoted to his family and profession. He worked long hours to build the newspaper in this community. I was blessed to be one of Dad's closest confidants. He typed letters to me two or three times a week for years, and we talked on the phone a lot. He led a rich life up until he saw his independence threatened as he became weakened by prostate cancer. Facing permanent nursing home care, he chose instead to end his life. It is a decision I cannot criticize. Many times during recent years, he talked about not wanting to be a burden to his family.

Henry Mead was a proud, principled, and literate man who read voraciously. He had a dozen hours of poetry committed to memory and was a commanding public speaker. He wrote clearly and eloquently. He loved the English language, and could he spell. When he was seventy, he took up a new career as an actor in a show he wrote about William Sydney Porter, better known by his pen name O. Henry, whom some call the master of the short story. He performed as O. Henry to more than a hundred audiences across the country. In 1989, when he was eighty-one, he wrote a script for a one-man show about Winston Churchill.

Curt concluded by reading one of Dad's favorite poems, *Do Not Go Gentle into That Good Night*, by Dylan Thomas. Here are the first few lines:

Do not go gentle into that good night,
Old age should burn and rave at close of day;
Rage, rage against the dying of the light.

It was a whole new world for me without him. There was no one who completely and lovingly understood, as he did, my hopes, dreams, and life. There was no one who needed me in quite the same way. He'd lived a long and productive life and, in his words, "wanted to check out painless and pronto rather than diapered and drooling in a nursing home." Some said his act was courageous. He saw his quality of life waning and wanted to move on yonder on his own terms. Had a "Death with Dignity" law been in effect as in Washington and Oregon, he would have taken that route and been spared from suicide. (Washington's law allows terminally ill adults seeking to end their life to request lethal doses of medication from medical and osteopathic physicians. Patients must be Washington residents and have less than six months to live.)

I idolized him all my life, and then he took his life. Dad had not been depressed during most of his life—that I was aware of—until his last years. Not wanting to be dependent is not the same as being depressed. My father was my most important role model, so it was a deep personal crisis when his death was suicide. What can you say about a man who had obituaries printed in fourteen different places? My idol's feet had turned to clay, and my image of him crumbled.

His death plunged me into deep darkness. I had never lost anyone so close before, and suicide made the struggle all the more difficult. I was in the darkest, scariest place I'd ever been—closer to the very thing that could annihilate me and what I feared most, the potential for my own suicide.

I found some comfort in going through his papers and finding stories he wrote and stories others had written about him. Here's a letter I found that he had written to a friend:

> Evonne has been elected treasurer of the Minnesota Press Association, and we are very proud of her as she is the first woman to be elected as an officer. As the tradition goes, she will eventually move to the president's spot and become the first woman in that role. So, I mused to her that in these days of equal opportunity and affirmative action, to say nothing of E. Pluribus Unum, Magna Carta, and habeas corpus, the nominating committee probably would have preferred, in addition to finding a talented woman, one who was black, Jewish, and handicapped. I suggested that, in her case, her doting father might qualify as her handicap.

I found a newspaper clipping from the *Omaha World-Herald* reminding me of another time. In 1971, while I was living in Germany, my father—thanks to the urging of my mother—hired his first woman editor, Marjane Ambler, who became an adopted daughter to my parents and a sister to me. Nearly fifteen years later, when my dad was seventy-six, Ambler wrote a feature about him for the *World-Herald's Magazine of the Midlands*. For years, our family would laugh about the way Ambler described my father's physique.

Henry Mead in his basement office in Seward, Nebr.

She wrote, "When I arrived in Nebraska to assume my duties, I got my first look at the man who came to influence my career the most. Mead wore his silver hair in a crew cut then, which was certainly outdated, even in rural Nebraska in 1971. But it suited his clipped, efficient, almost military manner. No one would call him plump; he never indulges in liquor or candy. Yet he looks round, rather like a sturdy oatmeal box."

My father had a fascinating and satisfying life in many ways. In 1948, as editor and part owner of the *Aitkin Independent Age,* he was riding on a train headed to a national newspaper meeting in Chicago when he overheard a man say he wanted to sell his newspaper. The man was William H. Smith and his paper was the *Seward County Independent.* That chance meeting between Smith and my Dad became a milestone in my family's life.

By the next year, dad had amassed a small amount of cash and enough reputation to convince John W. Cattle, Sr. at Cattle Bank to give him a loan to buy the Seward paper. Forty-three years later, in 1992, at age eighty-four, he was inducted into the Nebraska Newspaper Hall of Fame. He was a self-made, Horatio Alger-styled father with the failed son—the failed son who never got his life back after his hospital committal. Dad was a man with strong principles and great humor and concerned more about his children and what they made of their lives than money.

When Dad was seventy-four, the *Mille Lacs Messenger* in Isle, Minnesota, featured him in a story by Jay Andersen. Here are some excerpts:

> Henry is a story-teller, which is why he admires O. Henry. He saw one-man shows about Teddy Roosevelt, Harry Truman, Mark Twain, Will Rogers, Clarence Darrow and Emily Dickenson and decided he could do the same with O. Henry. Henry had read everything written by or published about O. Henry and created a one-man show about the author's life where he recited from memory about a half dozen O. Henry stories.
>
> Henry got his first newspaper job in 1924 at age thirteen where he earned twenty-one cents an hour, setting type by hand for the Isle paper which had a circulation of about 300.
>
> He was proud of his more than a hundred O. Henry shows he'd given throughout the country—at the peak, he averaged

three a month. The quick-witted Mead claims to have received as payment everything from a slice of apple pie to $125. He does it for the love of words. Henry is a taskmaster of the English language.

After Dad's death, Curt wrote from Boston:

> As you work on Dad's estate, I should tell you that in the long run, I have no interest in the *Aitkin Independent Age*. It might be best if I sell you my stock, but there is no urgency. I suspect I will be making changes in my life in the months ahead—perhaps going to Europe to live. I think I'm dealing with Father's death fairly well. There are moments when I feel an awful sinking feeling, but he is at peace now. I miss the letters, as I'm sure you do, too.
> Love,
> Curt

My life was getting better. I was doing some good work at my office but also taking time to grieve—less frequently now—so I called it progress. Sessions with my shrink were good. I moved along, but I was still angry and thought I always would be at some level.

Curt wrote from Seward that fall:

> It's been more of a challenge returning here than I anticipated, but I'm satisfied I did the right thing. I visit Mother every day [in the nursing home] and bring her two pieces of candy. I hold her hand, and we watch the TV news. I tell her I love her. I'm doing my duty. I'm salving my conscience ... perhaps.
> I think Aitkin would be better served if the paper were locally owned. I know I want nothing to do with the management of the *Age*, and I think the smart thing to do would be to sell it. Since it looks as if you're firmly planted in the Northwest, do you really want to spend the rest of your life trying to manage the newspaper from across the country?
> If you want to continue owning the *Age*, that's fine with me, but I hope you'll agree to buy my stock. Ownership implies responsibility, and I could never feel comfortable with income derived from a small-town newspaper in one of the poorest counties in the state. Think about how best I could get out of the *Age* in a way that would be comfortable for you. I think you might be tempted to continue ownership out of sentiment or sense of duty to Pop. Both would be wrong.

I'm arranging to take Mother to the country club for lunch with some of her friends as we've done in the past. I put it on her calendar, and it's something she looks forward to as she will your visit in November. I go to the gym every day and work on my plays and essays. I am hopeful.
Love,
Curt

The next month, he wrote:

Happy Birthday. I hope the books bring a chuckle or two. Margaret Atwood [*Good Bones and Simple Murders*] has her moments as a writer and P. J. O'Rourke [*All the Trouble in the World*] can be very funny. I'm glad I came here. I enjoy the panorama in the late afternoon while the sun paints the clouds as I return to Seward from the gym [in Lincoln]. Life is peaceful and secure but boring and banal. Have a Happy Birthday. I'll call you from Mother's room.
Love,
Curt

A few weeks after Dad died, I was watching PBS one evening and happened upon a newly released film, *The Tibetan Book of the Dead*, narrated by Leonard Cohen, the deep-voiced singer from the sixties. It was fascinating and gave me a feeling of equanimity about Dad's death in ways that my Christianity hadn't. That's not to say Christianity failed me, but rather that Buddhism augmented my spirituality. I bought the video and watched it many times. Later, I realized that film launched my knowledge of Buddhism, which became a great asset in my life years later.

I wrote to a family friend:

It's been a difficult time but Dad's suicide was not a complete surprise. He had been depressed for quite some time, despite taking anti-depressants. He told Curt and me many times about his wish to curl up with Mom and die. I told Curt his eulogy at Dad's funeral was a personal triumph, given the difficulties they had through the years.

It's a sad time because the most important person in my life is gone. Now there are no more letters in my mailbox from Dad but, instead, all the paperwork related to his death. An early reaction I had was that his act was courageous. Then I couldn't call it that, and now … well, I don't know. The past few years when he and Mom were in and out of the nursing home, I would share meals with them there. I remember watching Dad's expression as he looked at some of the residents and said, "That's not life. I don't want to live like that."

I responded quickly and firmly, "You aren't like that, Dad, and we need you and want you here."

~ ~ ~

One of the benefits of working for a six-state regional association of daily newspapers was meeting interesting, intelligent, and entertaining people. Jill Abernathy is one example. We met as professional colleagues and became fast friends, even though she lived in another state. She was seventeen years my elder and, for a couple of decades, served as a calm, gracious, and wise sounding board to me. She was a rock and guiding light through my challenges of parenting, aging parents, and romance as if she were my personal Ann Landers. She had strong opinions, quick wit, and a joy of life like few I've known. Jill was one of my life's treasures. Both lovers of writing, we would frequently spout off to one another in letters and later e-mails. Writing her would help clarify my thoughts. Here's an example:

> Dear Jill,
> Since I'm trustee and personal representative in my dad's affairs, I've been working about ten hours a week the last six weeks dealing with attorneys, CPAs, appraisers, morticians, gravestone salesmen, social security, and death claim forms from seven life insurance policies. I'm sick of it. I'm now majority stockholder in the Aitkin newspaper, seeking good counsel, and trying to be happy about the new assets. But I'm angry with Dad.
> Later lady,
> Evonne

Five weeks after his death, I had an incredible dream where Dad's essence flowed into me. Why did he wait so long? I read from my Bible, "Death, o death, where is thy sting? O grave, where is thy victory?"

To which I added … Grief, o grief, where is thy relief?

Six weeks since Dad's death. Buckets of tears. I've worked sixty hours dealing with his matters along with bad PMS. What do you do when you lose your best friend?

The death certificates finally arrived, and I spent my weekend completing forms and working on the appraisals. It wasn't fun. I dreamed of weekends in the rainforest. I knew they would come again, but now I had to do the business of Henry Mead. *What stage of grief am I in now? I've gone through shock, anger, denial and acceptance.* I was developing a new perspective, seeing Dad in the big picture.

I was having so many dreams—most I didn't remember but awakened, thinking they were important and helpful. *Yes, I will soar again. I will live, love, laugh, and learn. I will be creative.* Out of this grief, there would come new life. Processing. Processing. I had to face it—deal with it.

One day felt like a turning point when I was emotionally and physically at a low point and then bounced back into a more positive world. I had completed the final insurance claim form—maybe that had caused the change. All that was left was the appraisal of the *Age.* Good days. Bad days. I was slowly adjusting. Major progress at work, finally. Slowly got back into the groove. But there would be challenging days ahead. Investments. Keeping an eye on the Aitkin paper. Visiting Mom. Holidays without Dad.

With my regular job and ten hours of trust work a week, there was no time for a social life. I plodded along. Two months since Dad's death. I remembered saying, two weeks and counting, and now I could say, two months and counting. I was becoming a different person, thinking about immortality and what really counts. I would go to grief groups, back to Peterson, and the rainforest. I'd get into a regular exercise program again and maybe look for a smaller house.

I lost track of the weeks. That was a good sign. Seeing Peterson was good. It was good to get my work financials squared away. I was dealing with things better and time was healing me; I could feel it.

A trip to New England, then Spokane, and finally back home. Decompression. *Dad is dead.* Attorneys. Notaries. Documents. Signatures. Copying. Mailing. Paying Bills. Keeping it together. Making reservations, plans, planes, hotels, dates, times, places. TMJ (temporomandibular joint) pain returned after two decades of remission. I took sick leave. I took vacation.

Dad, you can't be gone. I don't want you gone. If I were to die tomorrow, what would my life mean? What can my life mean? What can I contribute? A perspective? An attitude? A change? Challenges. Transition. Deep thought and search. So much work, so many hours in putting Dad's estate to rest. When would it end? Had phone calls with Morris, Zimmerman, Morgan, Bolitho, and Hardy. Ugh. What about Aitkin? I think I want to keep the paper and be somewhat involved as I've always been.

I had a freeing and enlightening session with Peterson where I felt a changing perspective. I allowed myself to slow down after completing a big work project and realized how important that was for my well-being. I was working hard at getting balance in my life. I got two great books from Curt and a very touching—perhaps the last—birthday card from Mom.

My forty-seventh birthday. I thought about my life and options. I wanted to read and write more. Relax and exercise more. Take better care. Learn not to be so hard on myself. *How do I reason with these little guys who sit on my shoulders? How about start by getting to know them?*

In January 1996, Curt returned to Seward and wrote:

> I'm glad I came here. Nebraskans are ecstatic about their national football championship. Lives so devoid of individual achievement find such jubilance in the victory of their football team. How pathetic—as if they had done something other than sit in front of their television sets. There is so much here that distresses me. All the fat people. All the dull conversations I overhear in public. The banality of the local television news. The mediocrity of the advertising and journalism. The dullness of it all. My affliction continues to hamper my life with moments of great agony.

~ ~ ~

Eight months since Dad's suicide. I kept seeing his image in my mind, his thick silvery hair and caterpillar eyebrows. I had always been my father's daughter—we treasured each other. For a while, I tried to become him, following in his footsteps and spending a decade of my life publishing the weekly newspapers to which he had devoted his life. He was proud, willful, and as I came to learn, flawed.

I dreamed I had to leave on a boat with choppy ocean water for a mission—all by myself, at night, without warning, and with little time to prepare. It wasn't fair but realized I had no choice. I could accomplish the mission, but I could not challenge the orders; I had to accept them. (It wasn't hard to decipher the message in that dream.)

I drove to Pt. Defiance Park to hike in the old-growth forest ten minutes from my home. I needed to walk briskly, feel the wind, and smell the pines. Why had Dad been taken away? It was overpowering. I didn't know what to think about where he might be. Maybe there are spiritual forces that save a person's soul. Yes. A force like the wind delivered my father to a state of calm and peaceful energy that I could not see but know is there.

My father was uncommonly independent with an unwavering quality to him. He could be harsh on his kids, employees, and anyone else who didn't conform to his values. It bothered me that he was like that. What made him that way? I surmised it was because his early life had been hard for many years. Dad was sometimes gruff, it's true, but he wasn't a tyrant. He was firm but fair with a remarkable sense of humor. As an adult, in conversations, I stood my ground, and I think he liked that. It reminded him of him. He was blunt, willful, and often convinced that his way was best. Over time, I grew to understand that. When I see these qualities in me, I try to recognize them for what they are and let them go.

In college, in the late sixties, I had experiences so different from his generation. But not unlike the jack-in-the-box that can't spring free from its confines, I remained fettered to my father—first as publisher of our newspaper in Nebraska for three years and later in Minnesota for seven years. I was still my father's daughter. I felt I'd made peace with him while he was alive, but that was before his suicide. How could I reach a healthy perspective about that? I felt ambivalent. I wondered about the mimics we become in the shadows of our parents.

Maybe his suicide meant it was time to stop trying to be like him.

I didn't know how to accept the permanency of his death—that I would never see him, that there would be no more letters, phone calls, or visits.

There was only a void—as big as the forest around me.

LETTERS AND JOURNALS

Human speech is like a cracked kettle on which we tap crude
rhythms for bears to dance to while we long to make music
that will melt the stars.

—Gustave Flaubert, *Madame Bovary*

After Dad's death, Curt moved to Seward and wrote to a college
friend:

I continue to suffer from the neurological affliction that has
bothered me for years. I believe I'm conquering it, but it's a big
part of my life and a real bummer. Nebraska is such a boring
place, and I'm not happy here, though I'm not sure I'd be happy
anywhere as I'm still unable to create prose of any value. I leave
tomorrow for two weeks in New York City. I may have some
consulting possibilities that would have me living there about
half time for the next few months. After that, I might move to
Europe, but a part of me sees that as an escape from things I
really can't escape. The political scene looks grim to me. People
seem to be more mean-spirited and banal. The O. J. Simpson trial
is such a travesty insofar as it's treated as if it were something of
great importance. The mind of America seems captured by the
shallowest and most superficial matters. In one sense, I probably
could not be more alienated from American life. It seems that
lives have little depth and that people are sad, angry, and fearful.
There's a decline of civility, decency, and thoughtful examination.
Enough of that. I hope we both have good years ahead.
Curt

Curt planned a move to Europe and wrote:

It won't be long now until I will be free of this life, free of this goddamn town, and free of this godforsaken country. I have enough money to live in Europe for a year without working. Nearly every day, I imagine myself on a plane heading out of Logan Airport. I will buy a first class, one-way ticket from Boston to Paris to Frankfurt. I will be among the rich and enjoy some of the world's finest hotels and restaurants. In Paris, I imagine myself inside the entrance of the Louvre, at the main stairway. I turn to the right and, at the top of the stairs, there she stands, the Winged Victory of Samothrace, the powerful, headless woman of marble with outstretched angel wings. In my dreams, I have seen my head upon that statue.

In Germany, I shall be beckoned like an enchanted lover to ride horses in the Black Forest. I will leave America, fighting memories of loneliness, brutality, and the ugly squalor of life on the streets. I will remember what America has done to the battered women, troubled teens, hookers, strippers, products of betrayal, just like me. I struggle to forgive and forget. To some of those on the streets, I was like Clara Barton tending the walking wounded. I was like Florence Nightingale, tending mercies on the crippled, lonely longing of the world. I was Penelope who buried Ulysses. I was Ophelia who kissed the cold corpse of Hamlet and watched him lowered into the ground. I was Queen Dido who buried Aeneas. Don't think I wasn't. I was Cleopatra who buried Julius Caesar. I was Beatrice wandering through hell with no hope of a Dante to rescue me.

But in the Black Forest, I shall be free. My black Arabian stallion and I will be one fused flaming spirit in the woods. I will pull tight the reins, lean my head on his, and squeeze my knees against his body. I will push my heels into his side and command him, faster, faster. I will feel his energy with my aching heart, and his power will heal my tender spirit. Energy and justice will flame as one in the woods, galloping in the soothing wind. I will feel strong, proud, and serene. Faster, faithful steed, faster into the searing, soothing, silent wind. We will whistle through the air like a righteous arrow launched by a noble warrior. Strong and true, we shall be sacred and free in the wind.

A year later, Curt wrote from London:

I'm living in the lovely Kensington neighborhood, not far from Kensington Gardens with Kensington Palace, Princess Diana's home. The royalty fixation is so appalling. I'm planning an October opening of my play, a wildly implausible and funny story. I've hired a part-time employee who will select a theatre, director, and a cast of five. I send a postcard to Mother every week and have a plant delivered to her every month. Sometimes it breaks my heart to think of her day after day in the nursing home. I'm hopeful and frightened about my future as a playwright. The wounds of my forced hospitalization and homelessness still bother me. It would be great if you could come to London for the opening of my play. Let's hope for better times ahead.

Love,
Curt

In May 1996, my son graduated from high school, and Curt wrote to him from London:

Dear Adam:

Your kind note reached me yesterday. You write clearly and concisely. I'm so proud of you getting into Rhode Island School of Design. I know you will be challenged and excited there, and I'm sure you'll like Providence. I thought about coming for your graduation, but I must remain here, writing my plays. I talked with your mom about your coming to England for a week.

I'll be interviewing actresses and directors soon. That is always fun. Let us hope we both have creative and fun summers. Again, let me tell you how pleased I am with where you seem to be as a young man getting ready to go out in the world. I wish you all the best.

Love,
Curt

A few months later, he wrote me:

Thanks for the birthday card and check. My affliction worsens, and the doctors have discovered a small area of diseased or damaged tissue from the brain scans. It could be quite serious. I'm returning to Boston where I'm scheduled for more tests and expect to return to Nebraska after that. I'm in a bad mood. I can't live in London if my affliction gets worse, and I'm not writing. I have found many of your comments about my affliction to be almost accusatory, berating, and preachy. It seems to me you should withhold your critical comments unless they are solicited. My own diagnosis is not entirely inconsistent with what the doctors are seeing on my brain scans. I simply do not want to

discuss it. So, I shall be back in America and Nebraska soon. Lucky
me. I'll keep you posted.
  Love,
  Curt

That fall, I wrote him in Seward and suggested I join him and
Mother for Christmas, and he replied:

Enclosed are a few books for your birthday. I hope you enjoy
them. I find it very difficult to be in the company of people for
more than an hour because my affliction is insistent, and my ability
to control the yearning to stretch and twitch has become more
difficult. If you must come for Christmas, be prepared for me to
be absent. I'm sorry. Don't take it personally. I just couldn't be
pleasant. I'm in a rotten mood and have no desire for company.

When I arrived in Seward that Christmas, Curt had left a note and
a stack of gift books:

Welcome to Nebraska. I hope you find some happiness
here. Things remain rough with me, which is why it's best that
I'm not here. I hope you enjoy the books. Merry Christmas. I'm
sorry I can't be more cheerful and sociable. It's just not in the
cards this year.
  Love,
  Curt

I wrote from my family home in Nebraska:

I feel as though I'm facing spooks, late at night in the dark,
when I look through the window in the door leading to the garage
and see Dad's big old maroon Cadillac ... the scene of his death. I'd
planned to be here four days, and now it's eight! Each day I check
to see when I can fly out, but a winter storm has me stranded.
Please God, send me home soon. I'm in a time warp, trapped in
Seward, doing my duty. Catharsis. It was surreal to sort through
mother's clothes, remembering the occasions she wore them.

~ ~ ~

There used to be forty-one accounts in my computer finance files
for Mom, Dad, and the *Age*. I've now closed thirty-two and have only
nine remaining—that's huge progress. The computer message was
poignant and gave me pause, "Deleting the account (Dad's *Age* stock)
cannot be reversed. Are you sure you want to do this?" I stopped for
a moment and said another goodbye, then whoosh, one stroke on the

keyboard, and it was gone. It was painful. As I read the names of each account, I remembered the people, circumstances, and work involved in managing it. Goodbye. Good riddance. On with my life.

A few months later, Curt reported that he was flying to Boston to spend a few days in the hospital. His condition was getting worse. He wouldn't say if he was going for more tests or surgery. I was steadfast in my admonition to respect his wishes. I called and left messages, offering to help in any way, saying he didn't have to call back unless he wanted to talk. We'd not spoken for many weeks, and it tormented me not knowing what was happening.

Later that spring, I wrote to Curt:

> My life has been full of change recently. I'm dealing with anxiety and depression so started a new anti-depressant, Wellbutrin, about a month ago. Too much made me agitated, so I went to a smaller dose. I'm having difficulty separating what might be a chemical cause for my emotions versus my self-talk and attitudes. Onward and upward.

A month later, I wrote to him:

> I'm so relieved that the worst of my deep, dark depression is gone. It's interesting to me that bi-polar may be the diagnosis. I told my shrink that I was surprised because I never felt I was manic. He explained that there are several types of bi-polar, and the lack of a strong, manic phase is not unusual. I really don't care what he calls it; I'm just so glad that those dreadful feelings are gone. Take care, brother dear.
> Love,
> Evonne

That fall Curt wrote from Seward:

> I'm sorry you've been feeling down again. I want so much for you to be happy. Are you still taking lithium? I have bad feelings about that drug. You should know that I care about you and that you have been especially reliable, diligent, and thorough in all the negotiations, legal work, and record keeping involved in selling the *Age*. I live in a state of constant struggle and wonder if I'm dealing with genetic depression. I'm learning what a worsening of my condition would feel like and am not looking forward to having it worsen. I'm seeing Dr. Johnson again [a psychiatrist in Lincoln] and will be, once a week, for a while. Let us hope

better things lie ahead for us, but for now, it seems we are both siblings in suffering.

Love,

Curt

I decided to begin downsizing my belongings and wrote:

What do I do with my mother's silver bowl? It sits in my cupboard and discolors. As I polish it, I think of how I'd rather be spending my time. I'll bet Mother Teresa didn't polish silver. Out, out, damn spot ... and as the spots dissolved, a decision was made—get rid of this. Sort out everything. Simplify. Day after day, I became obsessed with this because it made me feel freer and newer. I pondered my life, my future, and when I might have more time to read. Finished Thomas Moore's *Care of the Soul* and found new treasures as I continued in Sarah Ban Breathnach's *Simple Abundance.* She suggests looking at each thing in your life and asking what are the reasons to have it? What are the reasons to get rid of it? I dreamed of travel to Greece—for thirty years, I've wanted to visit Amalia (my foreign exchange student sister in high school). Why not?

What a wonderful treat I gave myself—a beautiful drive to Hood Canal as the sun was setting. The next morning, I drove to Hamma Hamma on the Olympic Peninsula and the Lena Lake trailhead where I hiked up two miles. It's my heaven—a beautiful forest, blue sky, warm sun, fresh air, and the thrill of pulling myself up the mountain. Most important, I read and thought.

As time went on, I considered issues involved in providing care for Curt. He'd been living in Seward for more than a year now, dealing with his health problems. He'd seen a slew of neurologists and psychiatrists, had brain scans and other tests. He told me his doctors said he had symptoms of brain cancer but didn't believe the abnormalities in his scans were cancer.

The doctors' best guess was that the condition was the result of elevated levels of four heavy metals found in his blood—for which there is no cure. Curt said the likely source was his childhood exposure to the ink at the newspaper shop—his arms, hands, and face regularly became heavily covered. Despite the facts, his spirit was good. He worked hard to convince himself that things would be better, but his life was pretty grim—he just watched TV. It'd been nearly twenty years since he'd had any meaningful work. I decided my role was to be supportive and understanding.

At least my career was going well, and I was named executive director of the association in 1992. One of my board members told me, "You seem much more confident and at ease." Futurist Paul Saffo was a hit as a speaker for the annual meeting of publishers. As usual, after completion of my biggest work project each year, I planned vacation time. Six days into a twelve-day hiatus from work, I wrote to Curt:

> You were right to encourage me to do this. It took four days just to stop thinking about work. I'm finding it heavenly to have nothing scheduled day after day and do whatever suits me. I've been reading, writing, watching old movies, cooking, exercising, meditating, and feel more grounded and peaceful than I've felt in a long time. I decided I needed some time out as I turned fifty. Time to think and relax.

New Year's Day 1998. My spirits were high. I felt successful in many ways and was aware of a new inner peace. I wrote to Curt and wished him well on his move to Chicago.

Curt wrote from Seward to a college friend:

> Well buddy, I'm moving to Chicago for a few months. I took a short-term lease on a nice place—enclosed is my new address and phone. I felt I had to make a change. My affliction remains difficult and painful. I'm sending you a couple of recent emissions from the occasionally creative mind of Curt Mead. You've been a better friend to me than I have to you. I hope I can make it up someday. Thanks. My love to your wife and children.

The next month, I wrote to Curt:

> It's been an interesting few weeks—mind-challenging thoughts and writing from you. We've spent nearly four years dealing with the issues of Dad's death. Selling the Aitkin newspaper was like experiencing his death all over again. But in weekly sessions with my shrink, I've worked on defining my life more positively. The growth from my recent years of therapy was built on the foundation made back in Minnesota with Dieperink. Those cleansing years of tears and personal struggle began twenty years ago and are now mere ashes in my memories.
>
> I'm feeling better than I ever have. Dad's death and then the *Age* sale brought me such profound sadness, but now, those

issues have been dormant for many months. Your writing on Dad's suicide and the tribute to the people of Seward stirred up memories again. More than anything, the recent letters you've sent are obvious signs that you're processing your past. Could it be you're finding some peace? How could it be otherwise? Your processing pushed mine forward, too.

In April, Curt wrote:

Suffice it to say that I remain in Chicago at a different address with an unlisted phone number. I'm writing a bit and seeking consulting work with large corporations. I'm sorry I had to stop telephone communication with you. Frankly, I found it too frustrating and irritating. I think you are more upset about selling our old house than you admit. I'm hoping that once the dust settles on the house, we can talk amicably again. I look forward to hearing from you by mail. Please send letters to my attorney in Lincoln, and he'll forward them to me.

A better future,

Curt.

My mind was spinning after returning home from three days in Seattle at a conference on newspapers and the Internet with attendees from forty-four countries. In my thirty years of newspaper work, I have attended hundreds of conferences, and this was the most interesting, challenging, and inspiring of them all. In many ways, I'd never been happier. My work was going great, and my new assistant, Maggy, was terrific. I was delegating a lot of work to her, and that freed me to do other projects.

A few days before I left on a cross-country flight, I flipped on the tube one night and happened on Larry King interviewing James Van Praagh, an unknown to me. His book, *Talking to Heaven*, was on the *New York Times* bestseller list for nearly four years. Looking for something to read on my plane trip, I picked up a copy. I was skeptical of anyone who claimed to contact those who'd died, yet his stories were startling and convincing. The book left me changed and gave me a comfort about death that I'd not felt before.

Little did I know how much that would serve me in the weeks ahead.

In April, Curt wrote:

> My writing gets a little better, but my affliction plagues me.
> I've been meeting with business people in Chicago but have
> nothing solid yet.

A few weeks later, my phone rang one evening, and the voice of a strange woman asked for me. There was loud background noise, like a rowdy bar. She said, "Your brother wants to talk to you," and then Curt was on the line. His words were slurred, and he talked loudly, briskly, and brusquely. He was seriously drunk. In all my life, he'd never talked to me so cruelly. Cussing at me for what? Profanity after profanity. Finally, the woman took the phone again and said, "You know, your brother's had a lot to drink."

"Ya. I think so."

Click.

A few weeks later, the sale of our Seward house closed May 1. But that wasn't the only big event of the day.

A Call Unexpected

It was to be a day like none other in my life, though I didn't know it at the time. I propped my legs up and nestled in my comfortable deck chair after dinner. I relished the beauty of the fading spring day. I felt peace from the gentle sway of the tall pines. Beyond the trees, the expanse of emerald green grass on the golf course glistened as the last rays of sun brought a temporary vibrancy to the colors.

And then the phone rang.

"Hello."

"Is Evonne Agnello there?"

"This is Evonne."

"Is Curtis Mead your brother?"

"Yes."

"This is Officer Ritchie at the Los Angeles Coroner's Office, and I'm sorry to tell you that your brother is dead. We understand you're the next of kin, and we need to know what to do with his body."

"What? What happened? Where was he?"

"He was found in a Santa Monica hotel room today."

"Oh, I see." In shock, I shifted into reporter mode—get the facts. "Was there any sign of foul play?"

"No, we ruled that out with the police investigation. He was in the Calvert Hotel. He didn't answer the door. They knocked and called and then broke the lock. Apparently, he'd taken a shower, crawled into bed and gone to sleep."

"I see. Uh-huh. Huh. What was the cause of death?"

"We won't have that until the autopsy report."

"When will that be?"

"I don't know. It can take weeks, sometimes months. It will be at least a few weeks."

I hung up the phone and screamed to the heavens, "Curt! No! Oh, Curt! Not Curt Mead, my brother!" How could he be dead? He was only fifty-two. His life flashed before me—the young, freckled, red-haired lad and, later, the slender, bearded man. The next days were a blur. I made phones calls, plane reservations and wrote a eulogy. I flew from Seattle to Lincoln and drove the familiar twenty-five miles to my old family home in Seward.

Just days ago, I had made what I thought was my last visit to Seward, sorting the household goods for an auction. The last I knew, Curt was living in an apartment in Chicago. What was he doing in Santa Barbara?

When I had said my goodbyes to the house the previous week, I remembered thinking the steps from the garage to the house had such a well-known feel, and now I would sense the familiar steps one more time. I would sleep in my old bed one more time. And I would say goodbye to my old Seward home, packed full of memories, one more time.

It was comforting driving up that last hill on Highway 34—my familiarity with the landscape was part of it, but it was also fifty years of memories from the community where I had grown up. The people there were steady, stable, honest, and neighborly. This was small town Americana at its best, and growing up there was among my most treasured blessings. There's comfort in predictability, and there were predictable aspects of life in Seward. When I grew up in the fifties and sixties, each noon, the fire siren blew from the courthouse square, and each morning and evening, you could hear the Hughes Bros. whistle signaling the beginning and end of the workday. And each Wednesday morning—for nearly thirty years—my family's weekly newspaper, the *Seward County Independent*, hit the streets. I felt a sense of safety, and frayed by my grief, I relished that. Yet, amidst all the familiarity and predictability was the unpredictable—the horror of the death of my brother.

As my eyes rolled over the gentle slopes of land, I remembered something Curt had written about the natural beauty of this area: "On the lonely country roads at night, nature pleases the eye, ear, and nose. She is simple and serene in the plains, fields full of food, the gravel snapping under the wheels, and above the cosmos stretches out forever, beckoning like a lambent lover at a cabin door."

I neared the top of the final hill and spotted the East Hill Motel, a landmark for more than forty years. Much of the landscape of this town had remained the same, and when I faced the awful nightmare, the comfort of constancy provided a much-needed emotional stability. The right turn on Columbia Avenue was automatic, and then the familiar and gentle cobblestone bumps were further evidence that I had neared my home. For more than five decades, I'd returned here from the far corners of the world, and yet so much had remained the same.

I turned left on Moffit and saw the home where I grew up—a stately, two-story, white structure where my life took shape from age four through seventeen. The house was built in 1890 on a quarter-block of land, full of trees where decades ago, Curt and I played with the neighborhood kids, the Bowmasters, Bocks, and Finleys. I liked knowing that my upstairs bedroom would always be there. When I finished high school in 1965, my parents built a smaller home next door and sold our older one. So many times, I'd come back for holiday dinners, laughter, and lively conversations. But today there was no dinner waiting, and there were no people inside, eager for my arrival. Today there was only sorrow.

I was comforted by the thought of being surrounded by family and life-long friends. It had been ten hours since I'd left Tacoma, and though exhausted, I needed to ignore that to plan Curt's funeral. I sighed heavily as I approached the driveway and paused to notice the beauty of the afternoon sun on the tall pines across the street on the elegant old Hughes property. When I turned my head back toward the house, I gasped.

At the edge of the driveway was a huge, dead robin, and the color of the breast, intensified by the glistening sun, was the same as Curt's hair as a young boy—a vibrant red-orange. I had come to my old family home for whatever comforts I might find and was greeted by death on the doorstep.

Curt Mead on top of the swingset in our back yard in Seward, around 1952.

~ ~ ~

Here are excerpts of the eulogy I read at his memorial service:

For the past ten years or more, my brother was in intense physical and emotional pain. After about a dozen brain scans over a period of years, all the doctors could say was that he had many symptoms of brain cancer, but no cancer was detected. Last year, a blood test revealed excessive levels of four heavy metals in his brain. The doctors surmised that the likely source was the ink that Curt was exposed to as a child in our father's print shop. The doctors said that if metal poisoning was the cause for his condition, the symptoms would only get worse and that there was no cure or treatment. That's not a good report card as you get up each day and plan your future.

Last Christmas, Curt quietly and somberly told me, "I sense I am coming close to my death." I was so stunned that I couldn't respond. I didn't know what to say or ask.

My life was enriched and enlarged by having Curt as my brother. Every Christmas, for as long as I can remember, I would get not one but four or six books that changed me with ideas that brought new depth to my life. When I was in my thirties and going through a difficult time, he challenged me to break my routine. "Take time to reflect on your life," he wrote. "Create new dreams and ambitions. Come to grips with who you are and what you want to be. Raise your sights. Say to yourself, I can be bigger and happier than I am now. Experience more. Learn to love art and knowledge and ideals. Go somewhere and let your dreams bubble to the surface."

Curt could be eloquent, but his words were sometimes scathing. He once described Nebraskans, in not so loving terms, as "people who worship football instead of literature, art, or history. That's pretty appalling." But after the sharp words, in a piece he wrote a few weeks before his death, he concluded, "Seward gave me security and a sense of community, and for those things, I am grateful. From my father, I received a love of literature, a precious gift few fathers give their sons. From the newspaper, I gained intellectual self-confidence and a devotion to free speech. So, thanks, Seward, for the kindness you have bestowed upon my family and me. Until we meet again, Peace in the Valley."

A college friend of Curt's, John Helland, also spoke at the service:

Curt was unique. He was a special kind of friend—one everyone should have. If you had Curt as a friend, he would do anything for you; and you can't say that about too many people anymore. We were all impressed with Curt's intellect. He was as well read as anyone we knew.

Curt loved to laugh, and we loved to make him laugh. He loved to have fun, too, and Curt saw a lot of fun in his life. He really liked to play pool. One story combining Curt's pool playing and his intellect happened at a local bar near the University of Minnesota campus. One night Norman Mailer, the famous novelist who was giving a lecture at the university, had sought solitude in this workingman's bar. When Curt recognized him, he showed no hesitancy and walked right over to Mailer's booth, introduced himself, and engaged in some stimulating discussion. At one point, Mailer mentioned how impressed he was with Curt's literary knowledge, producing a big smile on Curt's face!

Curt had a huge heart and cared greatly about people. As a favor to some of his friends at the fraternity [Beta Theta Pi], he would help them and sometimes even write essay papers for them. I know Curt wanted to please his father and always worried he wouldn't be able to. From all accounts, it was hard to measure up to Henry Mead. I also know Henry viewed some of Curt's methods of fun with displeasure and worried about him. But Curt made Henry proud with his successful political consulting career and lecturing at Harvard.

Curt was unique. I'll never know another like him. I'm sorry that he didn't have more happiness in his life, because he certainly deserved that. And all of us are sorry that he's gone before his time. But the memories remain, and I and other friends will forever cherish them.

At the close of the service, I felt a powerful visceral release, but then the pastor ended on a stark note that jarred me. "And now, the real journey of grief begins." *No*, my mind screamed. *I don't want a journey of grief. This is a bad dream, and I want out. I want to go back to when Curt was alive.* After the graveside service, I could tell by the looks on the faces of those who filed by for hugs and handshakes that they understood—at some level—my grief because they, too, had known and loved this interesting and entertaining man.

I remember the sounds of warm chatter and laughter at the church lunch after the service. Mom, confined to a wheelchair, perked up with the socializing. What a pleasant change from the tears of recent days. Photographs of the gathering show me with a warm and pleasant smile, surrounded by old friends and classmates. What an invincible façade I portrayed—peaceful and composed while inside my soul was wrenched in pain.

The day after Curt's service, I was in our family home making calls and finishing business when our neighbor across the alley, Mary Ann Eickmeier, called and said she had clipped the obituary from the Lincoln paper for me. I went to get it and, when walking back to our house, even though there was no wind, the clipping fluttered up out of my hand and down the alley. As I chased it a few yards, I realized this ground was the site of many childhood play times with Curt. It was as if his spirit was in the air blowing the clipping and he had chosen to connect with me in this way. When I returned to the house, I went to make a phone call, and the phone was dead. How odd that the day after Curt's funeral, the phone went dead. Did he know he would be dead May 1 and intentionally set the date for the phone service to be discontinued a week later?

When I returned to Tacoma, I was a changed person, as now I had no brother. The furniture and boxes from our Seward home were stacked about—bittersweet reminders of my family. These goods arrived when I was in Seward so I left instructions with a friend about where to place them. The first morning home, I woke and saw my grandma's old dresser, which had been in Nebraska, and had to think for a minute. *Was I in Seward, or was I in Tacoma?* I decided to play the video of *The Tibetan Book of the Dead* that was so helpful when Dad died. I'd watched it many times and never noticed until this time that the address for ordering copies was Santa Monica—where Curt died. What an odd coincidence.

Ten days into the month of May, I finally got around to turning over the page on the wall calendar by my desk at home from April to May. I was stunned and shaken by the emotional intensity I felt from the new photo—exploding, luminescent orange, molten lava.

May 1998 calendar image. Brad Lewis, photographer, reprinted with permission.

Somehow, that lava vividly depicted the change I would expect when Curt's energy moved from this world to the next. When I asked, "Where did he go?" I felt his spirit had landed wherever there was nature's energy. In a shooting star, the pounding waves, or molten lava—there could reside some of Curt's transformed energy.

The next day, I felt like a pancake. As I started to leave for work, my garage door died, the spring had broken. *Dead brother. Dead door. Must stay home for repairman. Dead door easier than a dead brother.* I ordered Curt's gravestone inscribed "Peace in the Valley."

I got through my board meeting fine. Then a weekend to relax and write thank you notes. I received a wonderful letter from one of Dad's best friends, Howard Smith, a former Minnesota State legislator:

> Dear Evonne,
> First, I can't express the degree of shock and sadness we felt on opening your letter. For you to get the blow for the second time and unable to have your mother's comfort given her dementia. Your eulogy explained it all so clearly, gently and completely. Curt, like Henry, was an exceptionally brilliant person and one whom many had the pleasure of knowing.
> But you, Evonne, are still here to sort out your life. You are the one to see how to build the future on the high ground of your heritage. Indeed, there is much to build upon. Like the history of building America, there are great highlights as well as fallbacks. Thank you for thinking of me as an honorary pallbearer at Curt's service. I did love that boy and felt for him when he gave the eulogy for Henry four years ago.

I had days and days of tears, but they lessened in intensity and duration as I dealt with the issues and processed my sadness. I wanted the pain to end. Over Memorial Day weekend, I would make another trip to Seward to sort through Curt's things.

In Seward, I spent a couple of days in the basement of Jones Bank, the executor named in Curt's will, going through his belongings—which were mostly books, perhaps a thousand. I recognized a few sweaters that had been gifts from me. It was eerie ... his clothes hanging on this little rack, surrounded by boxes. One evening after I'd labored several hours, I drove past the band shell, and music filled the air. I recalled how I had played my clarinet on that stage on summer nights when I was a kid, so I parked my car and walked up to listen. Though I hadn't lived there in thirty years, I quickly spotted my childhood friend Becky (Cattle) Vahle, who is a pillar of the community and at Cattle

National Bank, and her mother, Virginia Cattle, one of my Bluebird leaders, and joined them. (Virginia's husband, John, was the one who loaned my dad the money in 1949 to buy the Seward paper.) When the song finished, the emcee said he'd like to see how far people had traveled to get to the concert. In a quick moment, I was in the limelight, raising my hand and shouting, "Tacoma, Washington." In about five minutes, I had gone from dealing with death garb in a basement to being applauded by a friendly crowd of concert goers. Ah, the fun and richness of small-town life.

The next month, I dreaded another trip, this time to a big newspaper conference in Orlando, but decided to go because Curt would want me to get back to my life. The diversion would likely do me good. What an experience—thirteen thousand people from all over the world grappling to learn the latest. I was distracted from my grief and became eager to define my life ahead.

I was looking forward to no trips in July before leaving in August for Charleston, South Carolina. After that would be several days in Olympia and then the Tri-Cities—a lot of travel. Two and a half months after Curt's death and I was still awaiting the autopsy report. I guess the LA Coroner's Office was a busy place. I took a deep breath and realized that one of these days, weeks, months, this would all be in the past. If I were lucky, my life might have new depth and meaning because of these experiences. I'd probably know in the next few days. Was it suicide? Two months ago, I had told myself, *Tuck this in the back of your mind. It will come when it comes.* Some of his boxes would be arriving at my house soon. Going through his belongings would be another emotional journey. What would I find?

DANCING IN THE SUN

I have been in sorrow's kitchen and licked out the pots.
—Zora Neale Thurston, *Their Eyes Were Watching God*

When I answered my phone that morning, a strange man's voice asked, "Is Evonne Agnello there?"

"Yes. This is Evonne."

"This is the Los Angeles Corner's Office, and I'm calling about the death of Curtis Mead."

"Yes, that's my brother."

"We've completed the autopsy report and the cause of death was salicylate toxication."

"What?"

"It was suicide caused by an overdose of aspirin."

After I hung up the phone, the scream from my mouth was like none I had ever heard. The tone, pitch, intensity, and volume all told me I was in a new and frightening experience—the news that my brother's death was suicide. Now there were *two* suicides in my family—Dad four years ago and now my only sibling. *No, God, no—not another suicide!*

My world turned upside down. Despair surrounded me like claws, threatening to pull me under. It had been two and a half months since his death, yet the finally released autopsy report hurled me downward again. I experienced his death a second time, only far worse with new pain and fear erupting.

Now that I had two suicides in my family, what was my fate? After Dad killed himself, I read the statistics and remembered the graphs.

Once a family has a suicide, the incidence of a second in the same family is significantly higher. Now I had two. I shuddered to think what that graph might look like. How much does that increase my odds? I felt doomed. I was depressed, and now I had this family history. I'd tried nearly a dozen anti-depressants in the past twenty years, along with years of psychotherapy. Shivers rifled my soul. Curt's death now threatened my life. Where was the way out of the darkness? *Oh, Curt, damn you!*

I screamed and cried. What could I do with this news? I'd been back at work, getting on with business, and now was thrust into an awful pain. I didn't know how to cope, but if I could inch blindly through the next moments, then I'd be on some path. Before calling family and friends, I jumped in the shower and asked myself what would I do on a normal day? I screamed. *Normal day? I've just learned I now have two suicides in my family! This is not a normal day. Okay, then pretend—just pretend. Make a simple plan that you can carry out and that will be progress.* I'd drop my car off at the shop for some scheduled work and then go to my office. I could not fall apart now. If I drove my car to the shop, that would be a sign that I could function, but I screamed to the heavens, "Okay, God, you have to help me now. I don't know what to do. You *have* to lead me."

When I got to my office, I broke the news to my assistant, Maggy, and asked her to shield me from calls. It was just the two of us running the association, and I was comforted knowing she was so capable. I called my family and friends and was buoyed and blessed with support. This was a critical point—I was only hours into the shock, and I needed all the help I could get.

I looked at my calendar and saw I had plans to meet some friends for lunch. I eyed the corner of my office floor where I wanted to crawl into a ball and cry for days. I decided lunch with friends was the better choice. *See, I'm all right*, I told myself, as if saying it would make it so. Inside, my psyche was on thin ice; this was uncharted territory. It was a warm July day, and as we wandered through the Farmer's Market we came across some folk dancing.

A friend of mine, Matt Temmel, was among those dancing and, not knowing my grief, called to me, "Hi, Evonne. Come join the dance."

"No, no thanks," I yelled back, shaking my head. *This is not my day for dancing. No siree—I'm in a morass of darkness.*

Then something came over me and I thought, well … *why not?* And I jumped in.

Four hours earlier, I'd learned my brother had killed himself, and now, on a hot July day, I was dancing in the sun, spinning and twirling. I was light-headed, had stopped the clock and stayed in the moment. As I froze the frame, my mind spun far from the dreadful world. I was overwhelmed with the change that had brought this darkness into my life, but I buried my anguish—albeit momentarily—and relished that I was dancing in the sun. Curt would want me to do this. In fact, it was probably his spirit that pulled me into that dance ring.

He would do something like that.

~ ~ ~

The next morning—day two of the shock—I wondered how I could possibly function at work. Shortly after settling in my office, an important call came from a key executive at the association's largest member. I took a deep breath. Three months ago, I had written a short note in the association bulletin explaining my absence following the death of my brother. By now, my business associates would have every reason to believe I would be functioning. How can I possibly take this call and pretend that everything is just fine? *Okay, pretend. Just pretend.* I took another deep breath.

"Hello. This is Evonne," I chirped. Amazingly, like an out-of-body experience, I found myself responding with clear and simple answers, talking as though everything was fine—as if I could simply wipe from my mind that twenty-four hours ago I had learned of my brother's suicide. I was completely composed throughout the conversation, though thoughts of Curt drenched my brain. Some little angel must have whispered in my ear, "Atta girl. You can cope." When I hung up the phone, I broke into tears and then composed myself again. I decided, *This works: do business, keep calm, cry some, and then get back to work.*

Ah, but I was angry with God—*really* angry. I felt the type of anger Mary Gordon describes as moving "through the body like a jet of freezing water."

I screamed out, "Okay God, I know why you dumped another one of these suicides on me. You saw how I struggled for *four* years to cope with Dad's suicide, how I slowly and patiently moved through it and beyond. Then you said, oh, Evonne's strong now, and since she's already coped with *one* suicide, she can handle another.

"Well, bah humbug, God, bah humbug!"

~ ~ ~

How would I tame this albatross that was pulling me down and would be with me forever? Wallace Stegner writes in *Crossing to Safety*, "You can plan all you want to. You can lie in your morning bed and fill whole notebooks with schemes and intentions. But within a single afternoon, within hours or minutes, everything you plan and everything you have fought to make yourself can be undone as a slug is undone when salt is poured on him."

It was strange that I got the news of his suicide just a few hours before his belongings arrived. I hoped to find some clues in the boxes about why he killed himself. If I could find some answers, it might help mollify my anger, confusion, and depression his death was causing me.

I went to a new grief support group, and no one else was there, so I had an hour by myself with a bright, empathetic pastor. It was good work. Then I walked along the water at sunset and absorbed the beauty of Mount Rainier while the breeze tousled my hair and cooled my face. I decided the boxes could stay unopened for a while and that it was better to go hear some jazz with friends. I needed to nurture skills, gain knowledge, develop insight—do whatever it took—to chase away the dark shadows of depression.

Four years after Dad's suicide, when I was finally feeling I had come to grips with it, news of Curt's suicide came, and the whole murky barrel of emotions tumbled out again—only this time with more vengeance. More strength was needed to tame the awakened beast of suicide, now transformed into a two-headed monster. Each day, the steps were small. It was about finding ways to go on. You either find ways or you don't, and I decided to plant my boots firmly on the side of going on. Yet I felt weak, as if I had been " thrown forward toward the unknown: uprooted, buffeted, without any resource," as Simone de Beauvoir wrote in *She Came to Stay*.

I felt as if twenty hands were grasped around my throat, trying to choke me. I was numb, paralyzed, frightened, fearful, and unbelieving of this second suicide news. Nothing had ever prepared me for this. A huge pile of emotional baggage had been dumped on me. The trauma took my whole being into disorientation, this severe emotional blow. How would I ever get over it?

I wrote a letter and sent it to Curt's doctors:

> I believe that my brother, Curt Mead, was a patient of yours sometime in the past. He committed suicide May 1, 1998 at age 52. Can you confirm whether he was a patient of yours and, if so, your diagnosis? He was single and had no children, so I am the next of kin. Thank you.

~ ~ ~

The clock turned seven as I slipped into a comfortable chair in the circle of a suicide support group I'd found in the Yellow Pages. It was four days after the news. I eagerly looked around to connect and nodded one at a time to five others. I saw compassion and sadness on their faces and felt safe.

A woman began, "My name is Marilyn, and I'm the group leader. We'll start by going around introducing ourselves and telling about what brought us here. I'll start. I'm here because about a dozen years ago, my teenage son took his life and I've been doing group work now for the past three years."

Next was a tall, lean gentleman in his fifties. "My wife took her life nine years ago. She used a shotgun, and I was the one who found her."

My heart sank. Oh, gawd. Nine years? I hoped I wouldn't be here nine years from now. A perky mother of two elementary-aged sons spoke next. "My husband was at the peak of his career when he was struck with a rare terminal illness. After a year in a wheelchair, he decided to hasten his death and shot himself. The boys and I were downstairs and heard the sound."

It was my turn.

"Four years ago, my eighty-five year old father killed himself by carbon monoxide poisoning in his garage after he was diagnosed with prostate cancer and faced life in a nursing home. He didn't want to spend his last days there. But now, it's been just four *days* since I got the news that my brother's death—two and a half months ago—was a suicide, too. Now I have two suicides in my family."

I felt I needed to fight for my sanity, and as I spoke, I saw my hand involuntarily move several inches above the arm on the chair and then down with a thud.

"I will *not allow* these suicides to destroy my life. I'll do *whatever* it takes to get out from under this. Dealing with my Dad's suicide for four years has given me some understanding about this. I've experienced this type of grief before and experience has to count for *something*."

Driving home, I realized I had had a good experience. It made me feel stronger, and it was helpful to be among others with similar experiences. I was motivated and had the best of intentions, but inside I was scared as hell. I comforted myself knowing that as awful as my experiences were, at least I was blessed—in both cases—because there was no blood and I was not the one to find their bodies. What small and odd cheer I found in my dark mood.

~ ~ ~

Manic depression was the diagnosis on Curt's hospital committal papers. Still, it was difficult for me to separate his delusions from what could have been true. There's a fine line between what's plausible and what is not. Perhaps his experiences in the underworld triggered his delusions. If only some omnipotent being could go through the whole script and mark sections true or false—maybe then I could put it to rest.

I was experiencing the development of strong coping skills. I was laughing. I was talking. I was crying. I was understanding and accepting the lack of focus and slowing down in my attempts to deal with work and life. I went to pour some orange juice and mistakenly opened the carton and then shook it, sending sticky liquid all over the kitchen … but, it was okay.

It was better to flow with the feelings than to struggle when I was like that. Grieving is a balancing act between positive thoughts about the future and the need to feel angry, sad, and confused. I worked through that and slowly found peace. Curt and Dad were gone. Period. I was here. Period. Seemed simple. It was—but it was also complex. No need to try and understand it all now. Time would heal and bring new perspectives. I was trying to lean on strengths from my experiences. I'd gone through four years of grieving Dad's suicide; I had understanding, skills, and insight into the process and the issues. And, I'd had years of talk therapy with excellent psychiatrists.

I was looking forward to the next day's drive through the Cascades for a weekend in Winthrop with a friend. On Monday, I'd go to a suicide support group, another grief group on Tuesday, my shrink on Wednesday. I'd make it through this. I would.

There were many advantages to my experiences with suicide compared to others. I forgave Dad because I understood his reasoning. He didn't want to live in a nursing home. I didn't feel guilty about the deaths like many survivors do. I truly believed that I couldn't have prevented either of them.

What peace I felt when I read my letter to Curt on his last birthday:

> Dear Curt,
> I spent a long time reading the birthday cards to find a good one. Then I finally picked this because it expressed my thoughts. "Every little deed, every quiet kindness you've shown me." It reminded me first of our childhood and then everything since. So many times, I've thought about what my life would have been like without you as my brother ... your interest, concern, companionship, and the many challenging thoughts you bring me. You have had profound and positive effects on me.
> So, Happy Birthday and thanks for being a great brother. Thanks for encouraging me in psychotherapy. Thanks for being a great intellectual model and mentor. I do believe there is a place for you—a reason for you to be here now. I offer my strongest support and encouragement as you seek meaning and discover the contributions you can make in this world. You are bright and have great insights. The world needs you.
> I'm slowly, but surely making progress in my world. I think it's only going to be up from here. I wish you the very best. Break a leg, dear brother.

The clearest time for me to put aside the sadness I'd felt for my father's suicide was dealing with Curt's suicide. The searing emotional pain lost its sting when the larger issue loomed of how to preserve my mental health. So, I rallied all the strength I had. No, I could not let this happen again. When strong-willed Katherine Graham came to grips with her husband's suicide, she wrote in her Pulitzer-prize winning *Personal History*, "I acted as though I was brave and then I was."

During the weekend in Winthrop, I felt like a child again in the swimming pool, playing water games and floating on my back as the stars came out. I was working to see some blessings in this grief. One I saw bubbling up was character building. I would not have these strong coping skills were it not for these challenges.

Keep going. Just keep going. Somehow, some way, I will see my way through this. I went to two new grief groups and had hours of talking, listening, and crying. I felt secure and safe in those environments and didn't want them to end. I called friends for support and comfort, asking for prayers. I was a basket case at work. It took so long to write the simplest memo. *It's okay. It's normal. Accept that.* I felt great anger and then moments of peace and calmness. I was reading two books on suicide, learning how to experience the feelings. This was truly the hardest thing I'd ever faced. Yet, I remember thinking that when Dad had died. I took a long walk, but still felt like a zombie.

I woke up feeling good. I could now say it'd been a week, not days. I was moving slowly through time. I felt sad that Curt wasn't able to live a long, happy, and productive life. But, I felt peace knowing his suffering had ceased. Lessons from tonight's grief group: You are forever changed by the loss. How you are changed depends on your attitude. You will come through this with new depth of character and compassion as well as the ability to support others. I liked that.

I tried to focus on the goodness in my life. I prayed every day and found strength and power in God leading and guiding me. But sadness loomed and pulled. What could I do? *Feel it. Flow with it. Try to understand that it's a long process.* Personal growth does not just fall from the sky. I had to take some responsibility to direct my words, actions, and thoughts in positive ways.

Secrets in the Boxes

Everything comes together and adds one knot more to the thread of life.

—Pablo Neruda, *Births*

My first reaction was to freeze when the long-awaited delivery of Curt's belongings arrived at my home. I made the advance decision to open all the boxes and get a perfunctory idea of their contents before I settled in to see what I'd find. I counted three boxes of writing and correspondence. I couldn't possibly read all that at once … and didn't want to either. After thinking I was eager to do this, I left the project untended in my garage for several days until I mustered the courage to make a second sweep of the papers. I decided to separate his writing from everything else. It would take weeks or months to go through it all, and I felt compelled to begin mining for clues about why he died—especially anything he'd written towards the end.

I stared at the stacks and realized how eager I was to discover what could be the secrets explaining his motive, but it was too painful to deal with for more than an hour or two at a time. About once a week, I'd pull out a few folders to see what I might find. Letters written as late as a month before his death indicate he had serious plans for completing the manuscript for his one-woman play he'd been working on for several years. There was a letter to a Tony award-winning actress in Los Angeles to whom he'd sent his script. He was pitching her to play the role for an opening in London. "I'm currently working with actresses in Chicago to polish the script," he wrote.

That explains all the glossy 8 x 10 photos and bios of beautiful actresses ... and records of checks to them. He'd hired them to read his script. That doesn't sound like something he'd do if he were about to kill himself. A note he wrote to an actress in Los Angeles read, "Your excellent comprehension of the key components of my vision for this character—the tension between hope and despair and lucidity and irrationality—will be the standard by which I shall judge others who try out for this role."

Hmm. So, that's why he was in California. He'd planned a trip there. At the end, "Best wishes to you. I hope you continue to get parts that challenge you as we all struggle towards the finest we can be as theatrical artists."

It seems he was a bit full of himself, saying he was a theatrical artist. That doesn't sound like a man on the verge of suicide. Or does it? What do I know about how his mind worked—or didn't work—in the end?

Ah, but here was more ... an agenda for a meeting with several actresses on April 1, a month before he died. "After today, I expect to work with each of you at least two hours a week for the next several weeks. I want to tap your reservoirs of experience and hear your comments about what you find awkward in the script."

I reached for another page. Here he mentioned the character in his play, "Mattie is based on my own relationship with a woman—with a different name, of course."

Mattie. Oh yes, I remember her—the high-class call girl, whom Curt talked about periodically through the years. I think she was the one who died in his arms. Why did Curt have such a bizarre intrigue for the seamy side of life—from high-class call girls to the homeless?

The next paper I found was a pale green page with a few typewritten lines, obviously describing himself and Mattie.

The Courtier and the Courtesan

We were both pawns of the rich.
I served them with my words, and she served them with her body.
It was natural that we would come together sooner or later.
I advised powerful men, and she slept with them.
I wrote their speeches, and she listened to their complaints.
I was in awe of their power, and she was in contempt of it.

This was too much. I decided to go to bed. The more answers I found, the more questions came forth. What was the real reason for his death? What pushed him over?

I cobbled ideas from the papers, trying to see a pattern, trying to understand. Day after day, questions spun in my head, and then I had an awful dream about gnarly tanks. The next morning, I grabbed pen and paper to record it as I knew I wanted to talk with Peterson about it.

> I was in a forest walking on a suspension bridge high above a glacial stream. The bridge was made from rope and wooden slats and had a steep, downward grade. It was breathtakingly scary, and I wanted desperately to cross safely. When I was halfway across, the bridge began violently swinging, and I feared for my life; I knew I had to keep moving or die. I finally made it to the other side and saw a clearing in the woods with a gravel road where two huge machines—the size and mass of army tanks—were rumbling towards me. There is no question that they represented the suicides of my father and brother. The machines were anthropomorphic with snarly faces; they snorted and growled loudly as they stirred up torrents of dust. These devils most certainly had their focus on me and were out to run me down. I ran with all my might, but they were faster, so I scrambled into the bushes at the side of the road. They veered towards me, and I narrowly missed being hit as they rumbled away into the distance.

It was one of my most vivid dreams, and it bothered me intensely. Yet, as the frightening images haunted me, I tried to dwell on the fact that, after all—in the end—I *had* escaped the beasts. As I battled the suicide beasts in my waking hours, they also brought me torturously frightening dreams for years. I was uncomfortable with the recurring theme of danger in so many of them. I repeatedly tried to convince myself that if I got out of the path and wrath of the suicides in my dreams, surely I would accomplish the same in my waking hours. I decided I'd had enough of this death detective work and instead focused on my life and career. For weeks, I didn't read any more of Curt's papers.

The next time I returned to the boxes, I avoided the papers and unpacked everything else. I found a bag of things the police found in his room when he died. Hmm … a small stack of CDs and a portable player. I glanced through the titles—would there be any clues here? But there were no heavy metal death-wish artists—instead Dylan, Baez, and some classical. Then through the opaque cover of the player, I saw something red—there was a disk inside.

Eeeee. This must have been the last one he listened to. Maybe this would be a clue. I gingerly opened the case and out popped Annie Lennox's *Diva* album. I was unfamiliar with it and had other things to tend to, so put it aside.

The next time I approached the papers again, I wondered what I'd find that day. *Let's see, what's all the detail on this long typewritten note?* At the top it read, "Introductory Remarks for April 1 Meeting with Chicago Actresses." *Sheezsh! One month before his suicide and he writes this?* "The play begins with Mattie, the high-class call girl, getting ready for a night out as we hear the song "Why" from Annie Lennox's *Diva* album."

Oh, that was the disk in his CD player. I continued reading.

"I'd like to play that song now and have you listen carefully to the words as they describe Mattie's life and predicament."

Oh, my gosh. What are these words? When I listened, I found them pertinent and poignant, about books never read, words never said, and paths never tread. And the clincher, "Why can't you see this boat is sinking?"

I returned to his remarks for his meeting with the Chicago actresses: "While the song is playing, Mattie selects a dress and dances lazily to the music. She's wearing a tasteful black slip, holds the dress up to her, and stares in the full-length mirror. She is poignant and funny, sad, yet charming, looking at herself and a photo of her dead husband. She proceeds to her make-up and talking herself into the cheerful geisha she will be that night."

Another day, I found a handwritten note of sympathy from a Chicago actress whom he'd auditioned. "I'm sorry to hear of your mother's death." *What? Curt told this lady our mother had died (when she hadn't) to explain why he was moving to Los Angeles? Why would he lie like that?*

One of the most gripping documents was a piece typed on faded pale green paper that he'd written on his fortieth birthday. Did it describe a cozy gathering of family and friends? Not quite. These excerpts show a glimpse inside the mind of one man's depression.

Thoughts Upon My Fortieth Birthday 1985

Nothing seems to have had any significance whatsoever. Nothing has mattered.

There was a time when I served liberty, freedom, and justice—selflessly and devotedly. I prided myself as an honest, generous, and thoughtful man, but it has meant nothing. I know betrayal too well. Misery and loneliness have been my constant companions. I have been beaten and allowed to starve. I have walked on bleeding, blistery feet, and no one stopped to help. I have written hundreds of letters to people who never answered them. I have been insulted, abused, and humiliated. I tried to remain gracious and embody all that I thought was good. I studied science in order to build weapons that would end the threat of nuclear war. I studied medicine in order to discover new ways to heal minds and bodies. I studied art and history for solace and comfort. I have not had a conversation I enjoyed in more than a year.

My life is a grotesque and pathetic joke, perpetrated upon me by a world I am trying to serve. It is the saddest thing—my lonely, lugubrious life. Who perpetrates this horror? Who causes this nightmare of anguish and despair? And why? There is no meaning to my life. There is no significance to what I tried to be. I have cried night after night. Surely, something good would happen, but it never has. For what crimes am I being punished? What horror is this? My utterly meaningless and insignificant existence.

The suffering, troubled mind that those words depict helped me understand the emotional torture my brother endured. His death was a dozen years later. Had he felt this intensity of torment all those years?

Each piece of writing, each letter, bill, and note was a small window into his life. As I caught glimpses of his condition, my drive to know the truth motivated me to read more. I felt like an excavator, exhuming his life. I kept looking for what might have tipped him over the edge.

I knew Curt had spent several years before his committal seeing a psychiatrist, Dr. Joseph Nostrum, because he talked about him a lot. Nostrum was the doctor who decided Curt should be hospitalized back in 1979, so I was enthralled when I found a five-page, single-spaced, typewritten letter Curt had written to him about seven months after his committal. I was expecting an angry letter, berating him for his part in Curt's capture, but I was wrong. Here are some excerpts:

> Dear Joseph,
>
> I thought I'd drop you a line and tell you a little about the course of my grieving in hopes you might find it interesting and because, by writing to you, I can deal with these issues in a somewhat intellectual fashion.
>
> As you may recall, I learned from Heinz Kohut about the creation of people to guide me. I used to tell you that I often put Ted Sorensen on my shoulder to watch me write. And during the intense period before my hospitalization, I had him up there along with my father, Albert Camus, and Robert Kennedy. I say all of that in preface to something that occurred a few months ago.
>
> I was in intense pain and thinking about my estrangement when I began putting those guys on my shoulder. I added others and asked them all to help me. As I pictured each of these men flashing by, I felt an internalization of them into me and a presence that I immediately labeled God. The next day, I was overcome with a powerfully calming feeling. I was surrounded by a force, like empathy, only more complex and profound. Searching for an explanation, I asked a clergyman, but he was of no help. I turned to reading Gandhi and found that some of his descriptions of his quest for God, and apprehension of Him, spoke eloquently to my experience.
>
> My depression and loneliness, while about half as powerful as they had been, are still overriding issues in my life. My struggle to write is nearly over, and I believe I'm on the eve of creating work of some genuine value. As the depression lifts, I find myself having heightened powers of sensitivity to people and an ability to quickly understand their issues.
>
> I sent an emotional and loving letter to my parents, and their response was to call my sister and suggest that I was going crazy again. So, I'm not looking forward to a happy Christmas. I expect to start doing a great deal of productive work when I return from Nebraska. I have the feeling of a returning conqueror. If any of this gives you cause to believe that I should see a psychiatrist again, I hope you let me know. I don't feel I need one, although I'd enjoy talking with one. Of course, I acknowledge your skills; your work seems, from my perspective thus far, to have been spectacular.

I have been developing a rather uncanny ability to see people's potential and brighter futures before they do. When I tell them what I think, they agree right away—which means I could be developing into one hell of a politician. I have before me the dream of being an Albert Camus or a Robert Kennedy.

I have many financial issues, back taxes and corporate matters, but I believe I can handle them efficiently and thoroughly. I have done much damage to my family and am aware of how little ability I have, or will have, to correct the damage quickly. That weighs heavily on my mind.

I've been writing about veterans the past two months and hope to spend Christmas Eve with them in Lincoln and New Year's Eve with them in Minneapolis. So, my friend, I'm on my way to some wonderful place. I'm serene, content and listening to a "still, small voice within" as Gandhi said.

Best wishes,
Curt

Another day, I picked up a manila folder labeled, Heinz Kohut. Inside were several letters Curt wrote to the famed psychiatrist (1913–1981). In 1980, Curt wrote:

Dear Dr. Kohut:
My name is Curt Mead, and I think we should meet. My psychiatrist told me to read you, and I did, over and over, *The Restoration of the Self* and *The Analysis of the Self*. And, now that my self is restored, I'd love to give you my analysis of it.

I figure if a seven-time college dropout is going to write to one of the nation's preeminent psychiatrists and have the unmitigated audacity to suggest that he's got a new way to look at mental illness and healing, then the least I can do is make the damn letter a bit interesting, so I'm enclosing my resume.

We might want to look at why people create their archaic selves. Why could Hitler activate the grandiose destructive self of the Germans against the Jews? Hitler and Vietnam are two atrocities every moral man must try to explain before he moves on.

Respectfully,

Curt Mead

The next week, Curt wrote again:

Dr. Kohut,

I'm trying to find a new way to explain things that is proscriptive because I believe a political philosopher must have a vision of a perfect man or a perfect society when he sets out to write history.

I think the perfect society, perpetrated by Karl Marx, has more impact on the world than it merits. Terms he introduced are coloring America's political dialogue, to its detriment. I'm seeking to find a new kind of man, a new kind of America, which is why I'm writing to David Cohen. On the Holocaust, one strategy I've thought of is to invite comment on Sartre's explanation of the Holocaust. Do you know of anyone who might pay some printer from Seward, Nebraska, for a year or so to continue this kind of thinking and writing? What do you suggest I do? I'll try to call you for a meeting.

Respectfully,

Curt Mead

Three weeks later, Curt wrote:

Kohut, you unresponsive son-of-a-bitch. Boy, are you going to be embarrassed someday when people realize that I was right about American mental disease and you wouldn't listen. Am I going to have to pay to see you?

Warm Regards,

Curt Mead.

Then, what did I find? Kohut finally responded to Curt's letters.

February 28, 1980

Mr. Curt Mead
316 4th Street, SE
Minneapolis, Minnesota 55414

Dear Mr. Mead:

Thank you for your note. I can understand your disappointment at the fact that I had not responded to your recent
letters. But I must ask you, in turn, to think yourself
into my position. I am not young anymore and, in addition,
had to contend during the past year with a siege of
serious illnesses from which I am just now beginning to
recover. In addition, as I am sure you will be able to
accept, my priorities are with my own work, i.e., I am
struggling along on my own road to obtain further insights
into man's emotions and motivations and that I can, therefore, give only little time to the many letters and manu-
scripts that I receive almost every day -- even though it
pains me to realize that, by responding late and incomp-
pletely, I often hurt the feelings of valuable individuals.

Still, I can tell you that I read all your letters carefully and that I enjoyed them. You have a good mind and
you express yourself in a lively, straightforward way.

I am glad that you find my work to be valuable and hope
that you will continue to do so. For the rest I can only
say that the major task of your development as a writer
and thinker, in whatever direction it will proceed, is to
be done within yourself.

I wish you a good and productive life.

                              Sincerely,

                              Heinz Kohut, M.D.

Curt responded the next day:

> Dear Dr. Kohut,
> I'm honored that you wrote me and sad to hear that you've been ill. I wish you a complete recovery. You will always be a hero of mine. I fervently hope that the world gives you the acclaim I am convinced you deserve. Someday, when I'm running something in this country, I'm going to ask you to come and consult. How would you like to be a consulting psychiatrist to the City of New York? If I ever get to be mayor of that marvelous city, I'll ask you to come and tell me how to do it better. Best wishes to you. Shalom.
> Warm personal regards,
> Curt Mead

Another day, I found papers about Curt's work at a medical lab in Lincoln where he took experimental drugs to earn money. *Might the drugs have caused something to go wrong? I know I'll never have answers, and now that he's dead, does it really matter?* I decided that rather than launch an intensive investigation, filing FOI requests for his medical and police records, my focus needed to be making sure *I* would survive. I found clues, but no answers, and much of what I found brought more torment than peace. I wanted to see if I could determine whether he had been framed (as he pleaded for years), mentally ill, physically ill, or a combination. Could the Thorazine that he took at Glenside have altered him permanently in a menacing way—enough to push him over the edge? He'd never been the same since his two-week committal, twenty years before his death.

If Thorazine—or other meds—caused Curt's muscular pain, then my brother's life was a sacrificial lamb on the altar of advancing treatment of mental illness. What a price to pay.

~ ~ ~

I found a scrawled note to Curt about the tic, suggesting it could be Tardive Tourette Syndrome, from Jerry Rosenbaum, Curt's old friend who was in the room during the intervention. The top of the notepad read, Harvard Medical School. I wondered if Jerry was still there and decided to see if I might track him down for an interview sometime. Maybe he'd be able to fill in some of the blanks in the mystery of Curt's death. On the web, I learn that Tardive Dyskinesia is a reported side effect of antipsychotic medication. The symptoms are muscle spasms and tics—involuntary movements affecting the eyes, tongue, face, neck, fingers, arms, legs, or toes. A couple of years before his death, Curt said tests showed heavy metals in his brain though the autopsy showed nothing. Had the metals dissipated, or had he made this up?

Another day and another find—this time a contract for an apartment in Santa Monica beginning May 1. That's when he was to move in—instead, he took his life. *He wouldn't have rented an apartment if he knew he was going to kill himself, would he? But who knows what goes on in the mind of a man before suicide?*

A month before his death, he'd sent his play to John Katzenbach and agents in London and California. Up until the end, he was following his dream of being a writer. What caused him to take his life? What could I have done to prevent his death?

I was both happy and sad when I reached into a large envelope labeled Earl Craig. I was happy recalling how much Curt enjoyed working for this talented man and how much fun they had on the 1970 campaign trail in Minnesota trying to beat Hubert Humphrey for the DFL's nomination for the U.S. Senate. Craig had the aura and intellect of Dr. King. I was a college senior at the University of Minnesota when Curt got me involved in the campaign, too. I met Earl several times and was mightily impressed.

I felt sad as I was reminded of Craig's untimely 1992 murder in Minneapolis. I remember that January when Curt called with the news and how intensely our family was angered and dismayed by the senseless killing. Earl had gone a long way after his Senate attempt. He taught political science from 1970–1980 at the University of Minnesota and a half dozen other Minnesota colleges. He had served as chair of the Minnesota Board of Human Rights and president of the Urban Coalition of Minneapolis. How sad that such a good man was needlessly killed.

Another day and I found more writing—three short pieces.

Smart Town, USA

Well, here we are in Smart Town, USA—Harvard Bar in Harvard Square. We're all so fucking smart around here. Just ask them; they'll tell you. Many are intellectual ass-kissers of the highest order and come here to tell each other how smart they are. If you sit in this place, as I have and will again tonight, you hear people tell each other, "This is the highest IQ bar in America." They actually say that to each other.

Down the street is the famed Massachusetts Institute of Technology, MIT, which stands for Monkey in Tights. Murderers in Training. Masters of War. At this very moment, young men who will one day make new poisonous gases and intelligent bombs are diligently studying. All the smug smart ones go to Harvard—the same smart ones who got us into the horrible war in Vietnam.

My medicine is Johnnie Walker Black. I'm in a great deal of pain, you see. I snort cocaine and I smoke pot. Some days I drink Scotch nearly all day long. I've been thrown out of bars all over the world. Hell, I've even been thrown out of countries.

So, I'm outside the pretentious Harvard Square Bar trying to build up my courage to go inside. And why? To remember? To forget? I recall my old crowd. We were so sophisticated. So hip. So elegant in our tastes. Everyone was witty and wealthy. It was everything everyone desperately wanted ... but it was nothing.

Clothes and Cocaine

I'm snorting cocaine. I'm sipping Scotch. I'm smoking weed. I'm seeking solace. The coke pushes me up. The Scotch slows me down. The weed mellows it out. It's a fragile balance. It doesn't last long. I'm so goddamn scared. I pace. I yell. I sob. I snort, I sip, I smoke—I'm a total mess. About four in the morning, I realize that as soon as the stores open, I must go shopping for a new outfit. I'm like a desperate alcoholic looking for the only open bar in town. At Saks Fifth Avenue and Bergdorf and Goodman, people seem to know who I am and give me the evil eye. Down the street at Filene's Basement, no one seems to notice psychos like me. When I'm hassled in the shops on Newbury, I pull out a handful of hundred dollar bills and make sure they see them. That generally keeps them away. I'm not the *only* impulsive person who rushes out to buy new things; lots of people do.

When I get home, I try on my new clothes, stare in the mirror, and try to find something I like. All dressed up and no place to go. I'm finally tired enough to sleep.

Lots of times, I never wear my new clothes again.

Sticky Despair

I feel as though I'm falling, slipping into oblivion and sliding into a deep dark cavern from which there is no escape. Will I ever pull out of this sticky despair? I park myself on a bench in the Boston Commons and strike up a conversation with an alluring damsel who happens to be having come coping problems of her own.

"Well, I can't believe it. There is someone even more fucked up than I am. You need a drink and a friend even more than I need a drink and a friend." So we head for the nearest bar. It's about ten in the morning. She orders bourbon; I order Scotch.

"It's a hell of a life, isn't it?" I begin, and she chuckles.

I chuckle back and we both laugh. Others around stare—they don't know we're two messed up people, betrayed and bruised, battling only for a few small moments of connection with another human being.

~ ~ ~

A chilling thought came when I realized the timing of Curt receiving his medical records from the psychiatric hospital and his death. It took eight months from his initial request—nineteen years after his committal—and his receiving them. The paper trail spelled out an intriguing and painful revelation. In July 1997, he first requested his records. After six months with no answer, Curt's attorney sent a second request. A letter from the hospital on January 29, 1998, reported the release was pending approval of the attending psychiatrist. Curt finally received the report March 2 and was dead two months later.

Was there something in the records that alarmed him? Maybe he had some difficult insights. Did he realize that some of his pain was a result of mental illness? Did he fear for his mind and see no hope? Did the medical report force him to understand that he'd been paranoid and delusional? Did he realize that his twenty-year belief in a conspiracy against him was wrong? Could the Glenside report have been what pushed him over the edge?

I tossed the papers aside in disgust, realizing I'd never know.

Growing Up Owning
an Ink Barrel

The Nebraska wind felt cold and blustery in March 1999 when I flew from Tacoma to take care of some family business. After I visited Mom, ninety-one and in her sixth year at the nursing home, she needed to nap so I left for a walk and some fresh air.

I drove around the courthouse square—the epicenter of Seward. Our old newspaper office was still in the same place. I grew up in that shop, and after college and eighteen months in Europe, I returned to Seward as a married woman and published my family's weekly from 1972–1975. Twenty-five years later, I walked around the square and saw a dozen or more people I knew and greeted them by name. Most knew my family history, and I knew theirs. I drove down the hill to the swimming pool where I had pedaled my bicycle hundreds of times as a child. I drove past Hughes Bros. and over the dike road to the larger part of the park and stopped to walk.

As I wandered the familiar landscape, the only sound was rustling leaves tossed by the wind into swirls. As the gusts stirred the leaves, the landscape stirred my memories, and sounds of the past came to mind. I heard echoes of bleating sheep, mooing cows, and children's laughter—the sounds of the Seward County Fair.

I paused near where, as a child of eight, I stood by my father as he taught my brother, then ten, how to take photos of the 4-H livestock winners with the Speed Graphic. It was a large, boxy machine that used sheet film about four inches square. Before taking a photo, you had to remove a thin piece of metal that shielded the film from the light. After snapping the shutter, you'd replace the shield and flip the cartridge over to shoot the next photo.

As I watched, I knew that I, too, would someday take photos at the fair. And, it was a great day in my character development when that happened. The next week, three thousand copies of the images I had captured were printed in the newspaper. It was fun to help create something cherished by people in the community. And it was so simple—taking pictures of kids with animals.

My earliest memory of the newspaper was being awed by the mighty machines of iron and steel. Sometime around 1951, when I was about four, Dad moved the business to larger quarters on the courthouse square. It was a major event in our lives and the town. Huge pieces of heavy and unwieldly presses, linotypes, and other equipment were hoisted onto platforms that sat atop large cylinders and then rolled down the street at a snail's pace. Onlookers lined the streets as if watching a parade. Though young, I think watching that spectacle provided the framework for my understanding of the power of the press. At the time, it was the physical mass of the machines that made the town stand still. Later I learned that the real power of the press was more complex than moving massive metal down the street.

When I was about six, I had the job of putting stamps on envelopes used for billing. As an adult, I smile now when I think how my life's work really began with that first box. Sometimes, Dad had me hand out the payroll checks, which was fun because everyone smiled and seemed happy and it made me feel like some benevolent being. At a young age, it gave me a sense of how things work.

As a child, I learned a lot about running a newspaper by osmosis. Around our family dinner table, I listened to stories about events before they were in the paper. I learned about fairness and controversy. It wasn't always easy to work for Henry Mead as he could be demanding, critical, and blunt. I was annoyed by his sometimes seemingly constant negative lamentations about his employees' foibles—especially misspelled words and bad grammar. I think he wanted everyone to be as smart, experienced, and committed as he was—and most weren't. On the other hand, he would show his employees, friends, and family great compassion and generosity when tragedies or hard times struck.

Each week, my dad decided what to print and what not to print. Often our dinner table conversations were interrupted by phone calls from people who wanted to keep their names out of the paper. We'd hear his half of the conversation, "No, I'm *not going* to do it," and wonder about the questions. After he hung up, we'd hear the full story and have a good lesson in ethics. The requests were often to withhold printing the name of someone charged with speeding or drunk driving. These experiences molded my beliefs in consistency and honesty.

One evening, Dad told a story about the lady who managed the roller skating rink. She'd stopped by the newspaper office to leave a free news item about the party she was sponsoring for the high school senior class. It would be chaperoned, and there would be popcorn and soft drinks for sale.

My father had asked, "Are you donating the use of the rink and the rental of the skates?"

"Of course not. I'm running a business."

"So am I. And I have a simple policy: If you give away your service or product, we give free publicity. But, if you charge, then we charge."

"Well then, you can just *skip* it," the matron had flared with her parting shot. "Mr. Mead, I'd heard you were *funny* that way."

My father was an exceptional storyteller. He could take something as simple as breakfast in a cafe and turn phrases that left one chuckling. Here's an example:

> On a recent trip to Greensboro, North Carolina, Evelyn and I stopped at a highway cafe for breakfast, and I ordered my usual toast and tea. But when the waitress brought my order, my plate also included a generous serving of grits.
>
> I pointed to the shapeless white mass and said, "I didn't order grits."
>
> She looked at me, eyes blazing with scorn, and in a voice dripping with contempt and incredulity, said, "You *don't want* the grits?"
>
> I quailed momentarily but held my ground. "No," I said meekly but defiantly, "I don't want the grits." With the air of one who snatches pearls cast before swine, the waitress retrieved the

plate and disappeared into the kitchen. Wordlessly, but with annoyance visible in every stride, she returned and slid the gritless plate before me.

As Evelyn and I ate our breakfast, I felt uncomfortable the way that waitress had looked at me. I had spurned her grits, and she made me feel as guilty as if I had cheated on my income tax, committed indecent exposure, or voted Republican—or some other shameful act that would outrage normal sensibilities or flout the canons of acceptable social behavior.

Another of Dad's stories:

I always had the impression that the British were a people of dignified reserve, so I was pleasantly surprised when I was walking through Hyde Park in London. Many strollers looked directly at me and smiled broadly as we met. A few minutes later, I learned why. One genial gentleman glanced at me, stopped, and beckoned me closer. "I say, old chap, some bird seems to have made a mess on your shoulder."

Curt and Evonne Mead inside our television in the early 1950s.

My father, the omnipotent newsman, always had a camera at hand and took lots of pictures of my brother and me. One of my favorites is of Curt and me on TV. Actually, we were *in* our TV. I was about four and Curt about six when the guts of our set were taken to Gill's for repair. Curt and I crawled inside the empty cabinet where there was just enough room for us. I remember it clearly because it generated so much amusement for our parents.

As they laughed, Dad grabbed the Speed Graphic and said, "Hey, little bairns (bare-knees)," as he called us, "stay put and I'll take your picture."

As Dad pulled the large, boxy camera to his eyes, I lifted my arm to Curt's shoulder. Later, I realized that this was the moment, helped set in memory by the photo, when my funny little redheaded, freckled-faced brother was becoming a beloved pal—a bond that would last for decades. I was also learning that the two of us together had a special power that neither had alone.

~ ~ ~

My mother was a behind-the-scenes brain of our newspaper business. In the 1950s, most women didn't work outside the home, but Mom was a skilled news hound and excellent reporter and writer. When she was in her seventies, she wrote a chapter in a book, *Death by Fire*, about the devastating Moose Lake, Minnesota, forest fire in 1918 that she barely survived as a child of nine.

As I grew older, my dad taught me nearly everything he knew about the newspaper business. I learned to write stories, take pictures, and write want-ads. I became a whiz on the adding machine and at balancing the books—large paper ledgers with long columns of numbers. Dad

Evelyn Mead

insisted that bank statements be reconciled to the penny to insure our records were correct. Later I learned how to "do the payroll," which meant grasping new complexities, like taxes and why some people earn more than others.

I learned a lot of science working in the newspaper shop, especially in the photo darkroom, a tiny little dark space full of envelopes of powdered chemicals, bottles of liquid chemicals, developing tanks and trays, sheet film holders, and a dank basement smell. The chemistry fascinated me. It was magical to see images emerge on a blank sheet of paper drenched in a tray of photo developer.

In junior high school, I had a crush on a teacher whose photo had been in the paper and decided I wanted to "blow up" the negative, as we say, and make a large print. In order to do this, I recruited my friend Jean Cattle to help, and we decided to turn the Beseler enlarger on its side to project the image on the wall. The Beseler was a rounded metal device that stood atop a pole, balanced by a platform below. The negative went between plates of glass that were placed into a slot at the top. Below were bellows that could expand and contract to change the image size. I placed a sheet of photo paper in the designated spot on the wall, and Jean turned the enlarger. Then … kaboom! The enlarger slid off the table but, luckily, landed partly in Jean's arms rather than on the floor. Had it fallen and been damaged, it would have been a huge disaster for both the newspaper and me. I could not think of a more grievous error.

As much as I worked at the paper and as many skills as I developed there, it was always interesting to me that my father repeatedly told me that nursing and teaching were good careers for women and never encouraged me to consider his profession. His mother had been a nurse, and my mother a teacher—and this was the 1950s. My brother was taught the intricacies of operating and maintaining the linotype and Heidelberg while I was taught the simpler machines, like the Ludlow, the proof press, and the Graphotype.

One time, I decided to protest the inequalities I faced as a little girl. I knew something was amiss when I felt shut out by my father whom I idolized. When he took Curt to the newspaper office on Saturday mornings, I had to stay home and help mother with housework. I was bored dusting knick-knacks and thought it was a waste of time. Curt learned how to run presses, and I polished furniture. It wasn't fair.

One day I angrily demanded to my mother, "How come Curt gets to go to the office and I have to stay home and clean?"

"That's just the way it is, Evonne."

I stomped off to my room with teary eyes and hurt feelings. Why didn't Daddy let me go to the office? Why should I be given such boring tasks compared to Curt's?

I vowed that when I grew up, I would work to make things right.

~ ~ ~

When I was eleven and in the sixth grade, my brother—then thirteen—was featured in the magazine of the state press association, the *Nebraska Newspaper*. I imagine my dad had bragged about his over-achieving son. The story's headline, "Six A's on Curt Mead's report card," next to a photo of him operating the Heidelberg press (when I was home dusting).

No one ran a photo and feature about me and the things I was learning. The story reported that Curt was "in his fourth year of piano, alternates between the trumpet and French horn in the grade school band and, as a member of a string orchestra, saws away two hours a week on a bass violin taller than he is. The red-haired eighth grader is currently completing the assembly of an FM radio and is past president of the Methodist Youth Fellowship."

In junior high, with Wayne Ulrich's guidance, I helped start a school newspaper, the *Salmugundi,* meaning an assortment of ideas, named after an 1807 satirical work by Washington Iring. I later followed in Curt's footsteps as editor of the high school newspaper, the *Bluejay Buzz*. When Curt was editor, he wrote scathing and comical columns under the pseudonym Ignantz Goldstein, though everyone knew it was Curt. It was during that era when I realized that although my mom did a lot of behind-the-scenes work for the newspaper, she was never paid. And, no one seemed to mind or care; it was just accepted.

My parents' intense community involvement taught me by example to think about public issues. They taught Curt and me that we had to be knowledgeable and aware of the world around us and we had to be involved and care about the needs of those less fortunate.

A new gust of blustery wind brought another flood of memories as I wandered through the park thinking how lucky I was to grow up in a newspaper family. The dust in the gust brought to mind the smells of the back shop and the rhythmical sounds of schllooop and psshsshsh that came from the Heidelberg press. The schllooop came from compressed air attached to a metal arm which grabbed each sheet of paper and delivered it to the platen. Once printed, the arm dropped the sheet in a collection bin, and you'd hear psshsshsh when the suction was released. It was amazing to watch through my impressionable young eyes.

We usually bought used equipment, and a weekly newspaper and print shop required a lot of it. But, the Heidelberg press we bought new. It was shipped all the way from Heidelberg, Germany, and when it arrived, everyone in the shop and our whole family gathered to watch the men pry open the giant wooden crate. It was a big day in our lives and for the business.

My father beamed at me and said, "Maybe someday you can visit Heidelberg and see where this press was made."

Little did he know—or maybe he did—that he set a-twirl my dreams of traveling the world. (How interesting that years later I lived and worked in Heidelberg my first year out of college, met my husband-to-be in that fairy-tale town, and indeed, saw where our old Heidelberg was made.)

Of all the sounds that emanated from the machines in the back shop, the most unusual and intricate were from the linotypes. These complex pieces of equipment were critical because they produced the newspaper text—one line at a time—from pots of molten lead. When the operator stroked the keyboard, a rapid series of independent "tinkle, tinkle, tinkle" sounds were heard. The amount of time varied between each sound, a rhythm dictated by the speed of the keyboard operator. The sounds came from brass letter molds dropping into sequence. Once a line was completed, the tinkling stopped momentarily, and a metal arm, called the distributor, grabbed the line and moved it to where the molten lead was flushed into the mold when it would produce a sound like sha-oosh. A few seconds later, the linotype spit out one line of type, which joined the others to form stories.

After the paper was printed, the type was wiped free of ink with gasoline-drenched rags and then dumped into a huge iron kettle where it was melted into liquid by a gas flame. It was true recycling. Each week the names and news of the past week dissolved to become the names and news of the next week. The names of last year's 4-H winners, for example, eventually became the names of the new winners, except for the Coufal kids (Allen, Nancy, and Jeanette), we used to joke, who won top awards nearly every year.

At an early age, I realized that publishing a weekly newspaper was great work, but also a great deal of work. For many years, beginning in early elementary school, I remember listening to my dad talk about newspapering with his friend, Stu Bohacek who published the nearby *Wilber Republican,* and became one of my dad's closest confidants. Their conversations were fascinating, and I listened keenly to their lively repartee around holiday dinner tables and other times when our families would gather. Stu was highly learned and eloquent and spoke differently to my dad than most men; and Dad talked differently to him, too. It was partly because of their common role as weekly newspaper publishers, but it was also their intellect, advanced vocabulary, and humor. I heard so many big words for the first time listening to their banter. Stu later sold his "ink barrel," became a U.S. diplomat in Japan, and then worked for Voice of America in Czechoslovakia.

In 1987, when my dad was eighty, he published a small book, *Letters to Stu*, to honor his then deceased friend. It's a collection of over a hundred vignettes about interesting experiences he'd had, many written with his characteristic droll sense of humor. Most were from letters he'd written his friend during several decades of correspondence, and others were true reports of events in his rather remarkable life. Our Aitkin print shop produced about a hundred copies, and it was so popular that four years later Dad published a sequel, *Letters to Stu Volume II,* with another hundred stories.

I think his best and most entertaining writing was a series of about thirty columns he wrote for the *Seward County Independent* in 1972 and 1973, where he described his struggles to get the Social Security Administration to believe he had retired.

Henry Mead's 80th birthday party, Jan. 19, 1988 at Clark and Linda Kolterman's. On his cake, as a joke, every word was misspelled.

On Evelyn Mead's 80th birthday, her grandson honored her with a surprise visit from a man in a gorilla suit who joined us during dinner at a Tacoma waterfront restaurant. The gorilla amazingly spoke some Norwegian, Evelyn's native tongue. No one else in the restaurant noticed, of course, as the black furry creature carried a handful of balloons and pranced among the tables to find us.

One of the most memorable characters in Seward during my tenure at the paper was Harold Davisson, a walking textbook of local history. I suggested that he write a column for the paper about the interesting people he talked about so adroitly, and he took me up on it. As the columns collected, it seemed natural to produce a book, which led Davisson to write a number of books about Seward's history.

One of the biggest events in the history of Seward was the Fourth of July grandstand program in 1974 when Davisson announced plans to build the world's largest time capsule on the front lawn of his business, the House of Davisson. He confided the secret to me the week before the announcement so we could print the story in our special Fourth of July edition, which we handed out at the grandstand show moments after the announcement was made. What a coup—one minute, a historic announcement and the next, free copies of our paper with details of the plan. I was proud because it showed the public that the press had been trusted with a precious secret. The next year, the capsule was built and buried containing five thousand items, including a new car, newspapers, letters, gift packages from local citizens, a man's aquamarine leisure suit and bikini underwear. In 1977, Davisson got his wish when the *Guinness Book of World Records* certified his time capsule as the largest in the world. In 1983, when someone challenged his record, Davisson built a second time capsule on top of the first one. He put a car in this section, too, but this time, a beat-up 1975 model.

About twenty-five years later, I had the opportunity to talk frequently with him again as his nursing home room was near my mom's. Harold spent his last days on earth still writing stories for the paper, typing them on a laptop from his nursing home bed. He was a creative man with a bent for promoting Seward and did lots of good for the community.

So, come around Seward on July 5, 2025 when the capsules will be opened, accompanied, I'm sure, by a great deal of hoopla.

~ ~ ~

When I was co-publisher with my husband beginning in 1972 and for as long as I could remember, the *Seward County Independent* reported county commissioner meetings a week late. When big news happened from that robust body, everyone knew about it before our story appeared the following week. That wasn't the kind of cutting-edge journalism we young up-starts wanted to produce. The commissioners met on Tuesdays, our deadline day, when we were like lions in a cage until the work was done. We paced back and forth in front of our paste-up tables as we placed headlines, stories, and ads on the pages of the paper, sometimes until the wee hours. In the early evening, we'd take a short dinner break and walk next door to Dominic's Tavern for Dominic and Mona Ricci's convivial conversation and famous home cooking. But, full of youthful energy, we juggled our work so I could attend the Tuesday morning meetings. That meant that at noon, I raced back from the courthouse to my typewriter and wrote the story on deadline. I loved the challenge and saw how my writing improved under pressure. It was a great exercise to write accurate reports without much time to think about how the story should be put together. The headline and lead were the most important, of course, and that involved making careful judgments. I loved that part—especially when there were controversial issues.

Evonne Agnello in the 1970s.

Publishing the Seward paper for three years was a great experience. We moved to the top of our game, and it would have been easy to spend the rest of our lives there. But we decided to leave for an untold future west. A few years later, after I was planted in the Northwest and pregnant with Adam, Dad called with the news that he had decided to sell the Seward paper. His voice quivered, as did mine, as our lives had been inextricably linked to that grand enterprise for nearly thirty years.

It was a wonderful gift to be a journalist and writer all my life. It kept me reading, writing, and thinking every day—and still does. I met so many interesting characters and had great fun asking them questions. I was constantly exposed to the full gamut of life styles, incomes, and mentalities—a kaleidoscope of the human race.

Growing up owning an ink barrel—albeit a small one—instilled in me curiosity, common sense, and a love of learning. Memories remain forever of how my character was molded in that small Nebraska town.

Dinner on the Beach

Writing is a way of saying you and the world have a chance.
—Richard Hugo, *The Triggering Town*

One of my first impulses when I learned of Curt's death was to visit the hotel where he died. I know families of plane crash victims often travel to where their loved ones died; now I understood those pilgrimages. I wanted see the ocean view that he had gazed upon during his last days. But I didn't go right away. I knew I'd be in LA again, sometime, and would visit the hotel then.

Fifteen months later, I was in San Luis Obispo for the annual conference of Newspaper Association Managers and found myself with a free afternoon and evening, a rental car, and enough gumption to drive down the coast and explore. I visited several beaches and then continued south to Santa Barbara. It had been many years since I'd been on these roads and was surprised to realize I was only a hundred miles from LA. *Hmm? I could be there in a couple of hours, have a nice dinner, and still get back to San Luis Obispo at a reasonable time.* I felt a visceral reaction, and then my car seemed to have a mind of its own. There was no question where I was headed—the Calvert Hotel in Santa Monica. I was going to visit the place where Curt had spent his last days.

My plan was simply to walk through the lobby and picture him there. I was expecting it to be nice because Curt had very expensive tastes sometimes. I imagined that he'd pick a classy place for his going away party, his last night out before the lights went out on his life, by his own volition.

I exited the freeway and drove a few miles west. Once on Ocean Boulevard, I soon spotted it—just like the picture on the web site. I parked and stared at it from a distance. Time started to slow down. If I didn't want to do this, I could just get back in the car and leave. But I didn't hesitate; I was on a mission now. I walked along the boulevard, breathed the fresh salty air in the gentle ocean breeze, and was lulled by the faint crash of waves upon the shore. I looked up and counted the floors to see the window of the room where Curt had died. I knew which one it was because a lady at the hotel had told me. I stopped across the street to collect my thoughts, take some deep breaths, and mentally prepare for what I was about to do.

The hotel was an old stone building with a small but stately porch with a few tables. Each was adorned with a vase of fresh flowers. Guests could sit in the curvaceous, rattan chairs and sip a drink, read a book, or chat while gazing at the ocean through a thin line of palm trees. It was inviting—I bet Curt had sat there.

As I neared the entryway, I felt I stepped back in time. The interior was dimly lit and elegant with swooping stone arches, a marble floor, and tall potted palms. I moved slowly around the lobby pretending I was looking for someone. *Ya, fat chance. Don't think Curt's here today.* Then I imagined that he *was*—seated over there in one of those plush chairs, reading a newspaper, and waiting for me. A deep breath surged in my chest. I walked past the front desk and down the hallway. *Now what?* A sign directed me to a lower level restaurant, but it was closed. As I walked back up the stairs, I didn't know where I was headed. I was outside of myself and wandered aimlessly as if in a dream. I found myself at the front desk, told the lady I was interested in a reservation, and asked if I could see a room.

"Yes, of course," the young woman answered pleasantly.

How quickly I continued my query, "Is Room 201 available, by any chance?" *I didn't consciously plan to do this. That was Curt's room.*

The woman swirled around quickly, grabbed a key, and answered, "Yes. Yes, it is," and called the bellman. "Will you show this lady Room 201, please?" The man nodded, and off we went. It all happened so fast.

Oh dear, I thought. *I don't want this guy with me. I never pictured it like this—some stranger with me as I visit the room where Curt died.*

Why didn't they just give me the key? The two of us walked into the elevator. The doors closed, tears filled my eyes, and a lump formed in my throat. The elevator started up and I realized I needed to tell this guy something to explain my behavior.

"My brother died in this room last year," I said calmly. "I'm from out of town and always wanted to see where he spent his last days." My knees buckled.

"I see," the bellman nodded, as his forehead furrowed and his eyes twitched from side to side.

The bellman unlocked the door, and we entered a small comfortable room. I walked to the window and saw the beautiful ocean—Curt's last view of the world. I pictured him there, looking out at the water, knowing he had decided to end his life. I imagined he made some remarkable farewell speech as he swallowed aspirin after aspirin.

I turned away from the window, into the room, and soaked in a memory that would be with me forever. I stared at the bed with its dusty-blue spread. That's where they found him. I wondered, *Were those the same pillows? Was that the bedspread that draped Curt's body?* I needed to leave. I thanked the bellman and walked out. *Okay. That's it. That's where Curt spent his last days. Now I can move on.*

In a stupor, I walked out of the hotel and ambled aimlessly down the street. Mission accomplished—my pilgrimage was complete. I'd have dinner before driving back to San Luis Obispo. *Curt, come join me,* I begged, *one last time, for a nice meal and good conversation.* But those times would never come again. I found a nice ocean-side restaurant in the next block and thought maybe Curt had dined here. We enjoyed good food, so I could easily imagine him savoring one last meal. Or maybe by that time he couldn't enjoy anything.

The maitre d' brought me to a lovely table on the outdoor veranda. I sat down and—despite the stunning ocean view—stared at the empty chair, picturing Curt there. My thoughts stormed angrily, *Curt, you could have been here! You were here, and now you'll never be here again!* As I stared at the chair, my ruminations continued. *Life is short. Life is precious. Curt was here and now he's gone. I'm here today but someday I'll be gone, too. Because life is so short, I must make the most of each day. I must. It has to be that way. But, how can I keep these suicides from poisoning my life?*

The waiter interrupted, "May I bring you something to start off with?"

I murmured to the side, "Yeah, my brother."

"I beg your pardon?"

"Oh, ah …"

Sorry, Evonne, the days with Curt are gone … and ice tea was a sorry consolation.

As I walked to my car, I took one last gaze at the hotel and recalled the words of Virginia Woolf in *To the Lighthouse*, "With her foot on the threshold she waited a moment longer in a scene which was vanishing even as she looked and then … it changed, it shaped itself differently; it had become, she knew, giving one last look at it over her shoulder, already the past."

Battling Depression

A harmful mist still remained suspended across the world, poisoning sounds, lights, and penetrating to the very marrow of her bones. She would have to wait until it dissipated by itself; wait, and watch, and suffer sordidly.

—Simon de Beauvoir, *She Came to Stay*

The experience in Santa Monica cleared one layer of grief but stirred others. My psychiatrist suggested I try adding another antidepressant, and I did. But after a few days, I called him.

"This new medicine isn't working. I can't take it anymore. It's making me nuts! I can't live like this."

"Don't take *any* more, and we'll talk about what to do next when I see you in a few days."

When I arrived at his office, I was angry and disgruntled.

"Oh, Dr. Peterson, I'm in a major depression. The damned enemy has returned; the battle isn't over. It's been more than a year since Curt's death—and five years since Dad's—but their suicides still haunt me. I'm afraid of this darkness and feel as if my life's at risk. How can I get out of this pit? It's as if their suicides are whirling cyclones in my mind and I'm caught in the center, battling depression and my greatest enemy, the suicides."

"Tell me more about your reactions to the new medicine."

"Well, I took one Thursday evening, and the next day I started having awful side effects. It pumped me up to a busy, hypomania stage that I've never experienced before. It certainly gave me new empathy for the mania I'd seen in Curt and a girlfriend in Minnesota. It became clear rather quickly the addition of the second medicine speeded me up too much. The side effects of that combo were worse than the condition I was trying to improve.

"It was hard to sit still, so I did a lot of hiking. I knew something was wrong when, leaving for the park, I was paralyzed, trying to decide which jacket to take. I decided that rather than waste time in this oddity, I'd wear one and put three others in the car. Another day, I was selecting menus for a conference and repeatedly read the options but couldn't make a decision. It was as if there was a roadblock to making choices. I threw down the menus and stomped to the phone—that's when I called you.

"So, now what? I counted back and realized I've tried *nine* different anti-depressants the past twelve years, and here I am at square one again."

"Not exactly. There're some other ways to think about that, which we can discuss later because our time is up today."

As I drove home, I thought, *Ah … just another day in the life of a depressive trying desperately to find the magic elixir for her unique brain chemistry. I wish I could say with certitude that I'll make it, that I'll be okay, that I'll be able to release the shackles of these suicides. But, God, oh God, how?*

Though I was in a dark time after the suicides, I made a conscious decision to fight. I would not allow myself to think that I couldn't be treated successfully. Instead, I would go to my grave, if necessary, trying new treatments, new drugs, more talk therapy—whatever it took—because I didn't want to live my life depressed. A depressive who really wants to change his or her condition has to learn how to not like depression. That sounds ludicrous, but think of two smokers trying to quit: one thinks it's a filthy habit, and the other says it's enjoyable. All else being equal, who will be the most likely to succeed? Telling a depressed person that a positive attitude will get him or her out of it is an insult—like giving a Band-Aid to someone with a broken arm. In my talk therapy, I reluctantly accepted that I couldn't simply talk myself out of depression by positive thinking. The darker the period, the longer and more intensely I searched for answers about this insidious disease—this beast of depression. How could I tame it? I was on and off lithium two different times. It worked for a while, pulling me out of the depths, but then left me feeling flat. I didn't enjoy happy events and decided I would rather deal with a variety of moods than feel bland about everything. I didn't want to live that way. I also didn't like going to the lab every couple of weeks for blood tests to make sure it wasn't causing kidney damage.

Then one day, hope sparked with a story in the *Seattle Post-Intelligencer* about a research program seeking depressed people as participants. Those accepted would have a tiny device implanted in their brains that would send small jolts of electricity to the vagus nerve—thus it was called a vagus nerve stimulator, VNS. It was originally used in studies of people with epilepsy to control seizures. Those who had their brains implanted with a VNS unexpectedly found a side effect of feeling happier. *Maybe this would be worth a try.*

I was at my wit's end when I learned about this, having tried yet another medicine that wasn't satisfactory. With such a history of unsuccessful treatment, I had moved to the point of considering experimental brain surgery. I shuddered at the idea but decided to persevere and trust that I would eventually find successful treatment, even if it meant brain surgery or spending my entire life trying every brain chemistry drug under the sun.

While "medications can be a miracle for many, they are no solution at all for others," Kathy Cronkite writes in her book, *On the Edge of Darkness: Conversations about Conquering Depression.* "So how do sufferers cope without pharmacological intervention?" she asks. I agree but would add, how do others cope *with* pharmacological intervention?

My doctor procured the paperwork for me to apply for the brain surgery when a lifelong friend told me about success she had with Serzone (nefazodone), and I asked my doctor about it.

"I hadn't thought of that one. Sure. It's worth a try." So, I began again with medication roulette and put the surgery option on the back burner.

~ ~ ~

I read in the newspaper about a Labyrinth Walk at a local church and decided to go. The purpose was to help you relax and develop a contemplative state. Walking on the path, you lose track of the outside world and thus quiet your mind, resulting in a state free of internal chatter. The experience reminded me that we all have only so many steps ahead. It's a limited number, and there are sharp turns where we're forced to change direction. At the edge of the labyrinth were tables and chairs with paper and pens, encouraging people to write … and I did. Here are some excerpts:

> I trust the Lord to show me the next path I should take in my life. My intuition tells me to make a change and not be concerned about what's next. Stop and smell the roses, spend more time with loved ones. I only have so many steps. I owe it to myself to make conscious choices while I can. Travel, read, write, volunteer, and take classes … so many options. Open my mind and heart to all the possibilities. Set me free to fly, to follow my deepest values. What would I do if I could truly say with gusto that I was living fully and to my potential?

When I arrived, I was depressed and in tears. When I left two hours later, I was changed and refreshed.

When the darkness was about as dark as it could be, when I was as depressed as I'd ever been, I decided there had to be other creatures on this planet who were experiencing this, too. I was not some wild mutant. *There must be support groups for people in this condition. Why not?* So, I found one.

As I pulled my car into the parking lot, I was full of ambivalence. The warm and beautiful evening summer air beckoned me to do *anything* but go inside and talk with depressed people. What a depressing thing to do. *Why don't you put the keys back in the ignition and slowly cruise outta here? Go take a healthy hike in the park. You know that's guaranteed to do you good.*

My conscience kicked in … *no, you've come this far; go inside.*

It was a large room with a flecked pea-green tile floor, a tall ceiling, and metal banquet tables arranged in a U-shape. Nothing too cozy or inviting. Kind of stuffy air. About ten people were seated, some in quiet conversation. There were chairs for about twenty.

I cautiously selected a place to sit—not too close to anyone, but not the furthest away either—a middle-of-the-road chair. I had come a little early but not *too* early. I didn't want to sit and stare, twitch and make small talk with depressed people. How would you do that anyway? What would you say? How bad is yours? And then hear, what? Stories of sadness? I felt highly unsure about this venture. I looked at my watch. With five minutes to start, I got up to find a restroom. When I returned, most of the chairs were filled.

I studied the faces before me and realized how normal they looked. I guess I was expecting that most would look down in the dumps. Some were frowning, but there were several with the spunk and enthusiasm you'd expect of the well adjusted.

Shortly after I was seated, a young man began. "I'm Sonny, the discussion leader tonight. We'll start by going around and introducing ourselves. Just check in or, if you'd like, tell us a little about what's been going on in your life."

I'll not share all the woeful tales of the troubled souls tormented by extensive mood and energy swings, but I'll tell a few—to give you a flavor of the evening. Several felt they had lost control of their lives, like Betty. She was a nicely appearing woman, about sixty, had a regular day job that she handled fine, a home, husband, and grown kids. But she couldn't sleep or even sit still very long. Her most heartfelt prayer was that she would find the right medicine or combination that would allow her to slow down, sit still, and sleep.

"It's been a bad week," she said. "Last Friday after work, I knew the weekend was coming, so I stopped by Home Depot and bought supplies to build a gazebo. This wasn't one of those pre-fab deals; I built mine from scratch."

She sighed heavily and continued, "Because I have this mania, I didn't sleep a wink the whole weekend, so I just kept working on the gazebo. Now I'm totally wiped out. These new meds my doctor has me on aren't helping—in fact, I think they're speeding me up—but I can't get in to see him for a couple of weeks. He's told me before that I need to try to stick it out with a med for at least a couple of weeks to give it a chance to build up in my system. He said the side effects during the first weeks can sometimes disappear as my body gets used to a new medicine or a higher dose. That's what my doctor says, so I'm hanging in there."

Then she smiled, looked a little relieved, and added, "Hey, at least I have a really cool gazebo."

Oh, gawd, I thought, *she's having serious problems. What a terrible predicament. When things get tough, guess we need to find simple joys where we can. At least Betty got some satisfaction from her project. What she described was clearly mania, and I thought this group was for depressed people. Obviously, it's for those with mania as well. My heart went out to her, but I couldn't identify with the mania. In my life, I've been depressed but not manic, and having seen my brother's mania, I counted that among my blessings.*

It was time for the next person to talk. Several in a row just gave their names and, though looking glum, said things had been going pretty well. One guy got up and moved to the back of the room where he could still be a part of the group but also satisfy his need to pace. Back and forth he walked, turned, and back again. I felt sad for him and glad I wasn't like that. *Is that part of the psychology of support groups, meeting people worse off so you feel better by default? What a desperate, bizarre way to be happy.*

Next, a man with mania, no medical insurance, and clearly needing help said that no psychiatrist would take him. A friend made some phone calls and got him an appointment with a doctor, but he'd have to wait two months. How would he pay the doctor and medicine bills with his poverty-level income? *Yet, this man could be the next Einstein.* My heart cried when I heard a single mom lament her awful choice to forgo her anti-depressant medicine because she had no room in her budget for the three-hundred-dollar monthly expense.

An older gentleman was next, seventy maybe, slumped, bony, and wrinkled. He looked sad, and nothing about him exuded good health. He told of trying to continue a medicine that wasn't helping and seemed to be making things worse. He was poor, had no insurance, but amazingly produced a smile as he looked up and said, "I was *finally* able to get an appointment at the VA but have to wait six weeks." He snorted, cast his eyes downward, and finished, "Maybe I'll be dead by then."

Oh, wasn't this a happy group?

My turn. I was cool. Dad's suicide four years ago, at age eighty-five, was okay because he'd lived a long and productive life. He just didn't want to spend his last days in a nursing home. Then a few months ago, my brother killed himself at age fifty-two, and it's especially hard because it was the second one. But, it's okay because he'd been in pain for many years and now that's over.

When I walked out, I felt strangely better. I'd gained a new appreciation for the struggles of people who deal with depression and mania and realized I was not alone. I drove slowly through the warm summer air and admitted that it was wishful thinking to say I was okay about these suicides, especially Curt's.

My entire being, character, and personality had been inseparable from him. If only I could have been there, I would have talked him out of it. I could have. At least, I would have made sure he got help. I didn't pick this path, but I can determine how I respond. It's my only way out.

~ ~ ~

I read in the newspaper that Hamilton Jordan (JER-dun) was coming to town to talk about his new book, *There's No Such Thing as a Bad Day: A Memoir*. I'd always liked Ham's casual, yet forthright, style when he was Jimmy Carter's chief of staff (1979–1981). He'd also been a newspaperman for many years so he was my kind of guy. He became an advocate for cancer research, largely because by age fifty, Jordan had been diagnosed with three cancers, including aggressive lymphoma and prostate. He urged those with cancer to take charge of their own treatment. Jordan said, "I made a promise to myself that I wouldn't let disease limit my life."

Ah, that's what I'm working for, too. I don't want the suicides or anything else to taint my life. But how to get there? How to pull out of the darkness?

THE TAPPER

After Curt died and our family home was sold, I thought more about moving Mom from her nursing home in Seward to Tacoma. At ninety-one, she might live another ten years, and I couldn't ignore my heart. I was sad thinking she might spend her last days without family, and I wanted to bring as much comfort as I could to the end of her life. I didn't have those opportunities with Curt and Dad.

Mom was wheelchair-bound with a catheter bag, so moving her would be a daunting task. But I knew if she remained in Nebraska, I would simply get a call one day that she had died. I'd had two of those calls already, with Curt and Dad. At least with Mom, there would be no suicide.

What if she died on the plane? Or, if a stressful trip hastened her death, I would feel responsible. Dr. Jacobs said no medical reason dictated that she not go, and my intuition told me she would likely be okay. She was hearty and strong-willed, yet, her mood and lucidity had unpredictable fluctuations, and there would be risks. The trip from Lincoln to SeaTac meant a plane change in Denver where we could be delayed or snowbound. I hammered out the pros and cons with my shrink and then made the decision; yes, I would take the risks. In the spring, when Mom's name came to the top of the wait list at the nursing home three blocks from my home, I made plane reservations. I was ecstatic and empowered by how satisfying it was to have made the decision. The next day, I picked up the tickets and drove home for lunch. What a happy time in my life.

I threw the tickets on the dining room table with a snap and shouted towards Nebraska, "Hey, Mom! I'm coming to get you! We're going to take a trip together—one more big trip."

It was a tingly moment when I sensed something above me, which I perceived as the spirits of Dad and Curt listening and cheering my decision. I grabbed my sandwich, flung open my deck door, and moved outside to sit in the warm spring sun. I felt accomplished and certain I was doing the right thing. After lunch, when I was brushing my teeth, I heard tap, tap, tap, tap on my living room window.

What's that? It was as if someone outside was knocking sharply on my window. *How can that be? Who would do that?* The blinds were closed, and I moved slowly to the edge and peeked out. No one was there. How strange. It was such a loud sound. I knew *someone* was tapping on the window. It was a real sound I heard. I shrugged and returned to the bathroom. Again, I heard tap, tap, tap, tap. Again, I went to the blinds, baffled and a little frightened. And again, I heard tap, tap, tap.

As I pulled back the blinds, I heard a swoosh, and a bird fluttered away. A bird! A bird was tapping, not just a few times but intermittently for five or ten minutes. I was stunned. I had lived in this house more than a dozen years and never heard birds tapping on my windows. What did this mean? Why would this bird tap on my window?

Then I smiled. I got it. I thought of Curt and Dad again and sensed their spirits had come via this messenger bird. I knew they would wholeheartedly support my decision, but I didn't expect *this*. Then I remembered the dead bird on the driveway when Curt died. Today, this bird had come—this live bird—not to remind me of death but to cheer me on in life.

~ ~ ~

The time to move Mom finally came. I flew to Nebraska and hosted a lovely bon voyage luncheon with her old friends. Her mood and spirits were good, and she perked up with all the attention. She beamed with joy when I told her we would soon be neighbors. A dozen hours later, I was heartily relieved to have her settled at the nursing home near my house. Early the next morning, I awoke with a phone call from Mom's nurse.

"Your mother is having an event—shall we resuscitate?"

"Yes. I'll be there in ten minutes."

As I dashed to her side, I tried to prepare for the inevitable. *This may be it.* Instead, I found her calm and alert. Oxygen and an IV had stabilized her, and I rode in the ambulance to the hospital with her. She wasn't in pain and seemed comfortable, but it was clear the curtains were closing. Her doctor said she could live three months, six months, but not more than a year.

After six days in the hospital, Mom returned to the nursing home. She talked some every day, was quite observant and incredibly coherent at times. She understood that we were neighbors and one night asked me who I was going to vote for. It was a roller coaster. How could I prepare for her death? I tried to pretend it wasn't imminent. What joy to bring her some comfort with cold packs for her bleeding gums. I told her things to look forward to, and her eyes perked up: celebrating Mother's Day together next week and Adam's visit next month. I knew she realized I was there for her comfort.

The hospice program was amazing. I kept getting calls from new people. Matt was our nurse; Carol, our social worker; Pickering, our pastor. My mother was dying, and three people were assigned to us. I never knew it would be like this. Mom had been here three weeks, and we'd spent time together every day. The last time we had had this much togetherness was when I had been in high school thirty-five years ago.

My dream came true. I brought Mom to my home for lunch, and she stayed nearly three hours. We looked at familiar objects and furniture that had been in our Nebraska home and called an old friend of hers in Minnesota. I showed her the fire-tattered Norwegian Bible her parents had brought on the boat from Norway in 1887, and she nodded with a deeply serene smile. That Bible survived the great Minnesota forest fire in 1918 that nearly took my mother's life. It was satisfying for me to watch her look at her old dining room table and chairs, the mahogany hutch, and our piano—it was like being in her Seward home again. Ah, the joy of being with her for three continuous weeks. She spoke Norwegian for the first time in a dozen years.

My mother was slowly dying. It was painful and sad, but she would die with me close by. Her hospice nurse couldn't have been better. New priorities arranged themselves. Nothing else mattered. I would help her be brave, or—more likely—she would help me be brave. This grief was so different from what I had experienced with Dad and Curt … little wonder. This was the natural way to die. *Damn you guys!*

My girlfriend Jill wrote:

> Excellent thoughts! Listen to that hospice nurse. Forget counting the days. I love your phrases: ride the roller coaster, intense experiences, new dimensions, new priorities arrange themselves. Hey, lady … relax. You have no control in the outcome anyway. Ride it out the most pleasurable way. Revel in the now instead of future death thoughts. You know the outcome. Why dwell on it while the present is happening nicely?
>
> Think of all the people in that establishment who do not have advocates. I see it over and over in the hospital—people who advocate for family members get better care. Pleasant people with smiles on their faces, people who are insistent, people who are relentless, get better treatment than those who scream and holler. Onward.

I dreaded the day. As I was dressing, I knew Mom's death was imminent. Unknowingly, I put on my Paris socks. Last spring, I had bought some beautiful black socks on a trip to Paris. *Wouldn't it be grand to step into these socks and beam myself back to those pleasant days in France?* The playful thinking perked up my sullen spirit. I prayed for strength, courage, and peace and finished putting on my socks. Paris socks. I felt a deepening perspective on life and death. *Powerful, playful Paris socks.* They provided an escape to a memory that helped me face this day of death. *These little socks climbed to the top of the Eifel Tower and Montmartre, they strutted up the Champs-Elysees and walked the Normandy beaches.*

~ ~ ~

Mom's condition changed to a semi-coma, and she was moved to the "dying" room—a lovely, private space for families. There was a big easy chair, pretty wallpaper, a coffee pot, microwave, and even the ubiquitous TV. The staff brought in a bed for me, and I pushed it next to Mom. She watched me crawl in and then closed her eyes.

All night I stared at her, listening to her breath, watching her chest move up and down, knowing these were among her last. The next day her hospice nurse, a kind and caring man, came in and sat down to talk.

Mom was sleeping, so he whispered, "Tell me about your mom's life."

"She was born in rural Minnesota in 1907, the youngest of eight children. Her parents had come from Norway, twenty years earlier."

We stared at my mom's motionless, peaceful-looking face as I spoke.

"My parents had been married fifty-seven years when Dad died six years ago. They were both children of poor families but ended up traveling the world and all over the U.S. As a newspaper family, we were surrounded by books, newspapers, and magazines, which we read and discussed."

I paused, looked towards Mom and gasped. Her eyes flashed open. She didn't talk, but her expression was clear, "I heard you talking about me." She looked at me with a puzzled expression as if she knew she would soon pass through the pearly gates.

After the nurse left, I had a memorable couple of hours with Mom. We were locked in eye contact as I told her, "Follow the light. Don't be afraid. We're surrounded by thousands of angels. Pretty soon you'll be reunited with all your family, Hilda and Inga, Sam, Melvin, Victor, John, and Emil." I read Psalms 23 and I Corinthians 15:55, "Death o death, where is thy sting?" and how "we shall all be changed, in a moment, in a twinkling of an eye, at the last trumpet."

I told her I loved her. I held her hand and dabbed her brow with a cool cloth. Throughout the night, I listened to her breathing. When it became labored, I called the nurse who gave her more morphine. As it took hold, her breaths slowed and became relaxed. When the nurse awoke me, a chorus of birds chirped as the sun came up to beautiful blue skies.

"I think your mom's beginning her journey," she said. I saw her chest rise and fall with the breath of life once, twice, and then … stillness. It was simple and profound. The nurse took her pulse. Nothing. She tried two more times. I prayed for a miracle.

Mom, come back. I don't want to lose you.

But the inevitable had come. God gave her ninety-two years, and I'd had her for fifty-two. Every day of my life, she was there for me … and now she was gone. I had traveled and lived all over the world, gone months and sometimes years from her side but, in the end, God granted me the blessing of being with her the last six weeks of her life … and her last hours.

After Dad's and Curt's suicides, I was struck by the contrast of witnessing Mom's peaceful, normal, and natural death. Even in her death, she was teaching me. I shuddered, thinking that now she was on the other side she'd learn for the first time that both her husband and son had committed suicide. Or, maybe those things don't matter on the other side.

I went home to begin plans for her service. I knew what to do since this was the third and final time I'd bury a family member. With little sleep and in shock, I looked in the mirror, and my face blurred. It was as if I had two heads, one on top of the other and then one tilted to the side. I stared and blinked; there in the mirror was a ghost-like image of my mother's face, which then floated on top of mine and dissolved.

Like childbirth, it was one the most transcendent experiences of my life and I felt mom's spirit around me, chanting, "Carry on and enjoy."

~ ~ ~

During the first weeks of my grief, I felt a shifting of ideas and a slow ratcheting down of the pain. Though I felt no vitality or joy and inside was crying with angst, I put on an effervescent face in public and responsibly took care of my life and career.

Jill wrote, "Why can't you let it go? Why do you allow these dead people to affect you so? It's as though you're letting them rule you from their graves."

It was a piercing thought that blindsided me; she was right. These people were in the ground and we, still on top, needed to get on with it. I knew from experience that the paralyzing feelings eventually fade. I thought I had accepted Dad's and Curt's decisions and forgiven them. It was their choice, not mine. But Mom's death ignited some unresolved anger towards the guys. The suicides came bubbling up with a new vengeance, yet my disgust made me feel as though I was somehow standing taller.

In my family, we all had our spells of depression and negativity, but we certainly didn't recognize it as such, talk about it, or deal with it. From the 1960s through the 1990s, talking about depression, much less treating it, was not common. May that time be past forever ... now.

Mom, Dad, and Curt were all active, involved citizens in their heydays, and I think they stuffed their feelings through work and being busy. Growing up in this environment, do you think I played my cards any differently? But now, things had to change. I was working through the anger of the suicides so I could release it to feel clear and at peace. I needed to do this. If I didn't, the poison would haunt me forever. I wanted to move beyond this, but I had to cry the tears, scream, and expel the anger, or it would block my capacity for joy and love. I was struggling with my meds again. My energy was low, and it was hard to get up in the morning despite sleeping way more hours than normal.

Two months later, I wrote:

> Serenity is slowly sifting into my soul, and this sublime sensation is shifting my paradigm. I feel a change of consciousness. I'd been stunned by suicides and other struggles. I had gasped for air more than once with heartaches from failed romance. For years, my weekends were filled with work. Could life be anything *but* serene after resolving so many conflicts? It was more than just getting through the difficulties that brought me to where I was. I fought hard for my sanity. I faced the demons of despair squarely and shouted to them again and again, "I will not let you destroy me."

It was several weeks after Mom's death, and I had spent the evening curled up in a living room chair reading a book. As I got up, I noticed a couple of feathers near the throw pillows on the couch. I reached to pick them up and nonchalantly thought there must be a rip in one of the pillows and went to bed. A few days later, I was in the living room again when I saw more feathers—several more. As I picked them up, I thought, *Wait a minute ... these are foam pillows. They wouldn't lose feathers.*

I slowly turned my head, and my eyes swept the room. *Eeeegh!* On the carpet, a few feet from me, was a big, black dead bird and tiny drops of dried blood on the couch and carpet. I quickly fetched a bag, donned rubber gloves, scooped up the carcass with a newspaper, and solemnly carried it to the garbage. The last time I had disposed of a dead bird was when Curt had died. Now, two years later, a few weeks after Mom's death, a bird dies in my living room.

I angrily shouted upward. *Dead people! Dead birds! Enough of death for a while now, God! Okay?*

VISIONING

Experiences that hone our coping skills are celestial benedictions in dark disguises, sent not to try our souls, but to enlarge them.

—Longfellow

How odd to experience deep rage about the suicides after witnessing the normal and peaceful death of my mom—but then maybe it did make sense. In dealing with Curt's suicide, I had the experience of four years dealing with Dad's, but then my grief about Curt's suicide compounded my grief about Dad, and then Mom's death triggered it all again.

I sought so many grief groups that one friend in a writing class dubbed me a "grief group junkie." But with no family close by, I needed to talk with people besides my friends and shrink. I found a grief group for those who had lost a parent, another for those who had lost someone to suicide, another for those grieving from any kind of death, and a powerful, six-week program run by hospice.

I felt continually wiped out, depressed, and haunted by unfamiliar and treacherous thoughts. I experienced extreme emotional pain and physical tension—some might call it a nervous breakdown. When I seemingly fell apart and screamed to the heavens, it was something necessary for me to do to move forward. I felt it was not a breakdown—there was no diagnosis or hospitalization; it was a break*through*, a turning point to be celebrated because bad feelings had been released.

At one grief group, a woman, week after week, described her joyless life of debilitating grief. Her only bright spot was the pride she had in keeping her job, given her struggles just to get through the day.

These experiences taught me that there's a wide variation in grieving. After a couple of hours with other grieving people, I felt much better, the difference between night and day. How strange to find such good feelings after focusing so much on bad ones.

I was determined not to gloss over my sorrow knowing that, left unresolved, it could manifest itself in depression. That was not something I wanted to happen. I was already depressed and didn't think I could handle one more ounce. Though grief can mellow to nearly nothing, you can never make it disappear completely, as you might remove a spot from a shirt. The death of people close to us becomes part of the fabric of our lives. There was no way for me to get out of the darkness except to take as long as necessary to disarm and neutralize the stronghold of the emotional pain.

For many weeks, I attended a grief group at the Mountain View Funeral Home in Tacoma, where we met in a spacious and sunny atrium. The inviting décor was replete with tall, lush palms and thick, comfortable cushions in graceful rattan chairs. You might have thought you were in a Caribbean cabana, instead of a funeral home, except there was no sexy salsa music—instead a muted pipe organ. During the discussions, I cried and listened to others cry. How bittersweet to absorb the sadness of these strangers with whom I shared a common bond. At first, it seemed odd to have the grief of others aid my healing and lighten my darkness, but that was my experience.

Each week, the group leader, Keith, would push a cart full of books about death and grief from his office to the atrium. The titles described the stages and varieties of grief; they gripped me and beckoned me to enter their pages. Week after week, I checked out books and read about death and grief. If only I had enough knowledge, then the pain might subside. I wanted to understand it, deal with it, and be done with it. Yet, darkness and thoughts of death continued to swirl in my head no matter how hard I wished it otherwise. After days of tears, I was reading a book that described a grief processing exercise called visioning where I would need to imagine my family seated around me and tell them all I needed to say. The idea of talking to dead people didn't appeal to me; it seemed like game playing—nothing more than hocus-pocus. I needed something more substantial than an amateur séance to heal.

Then I had second thoughts. *Why not try it?* I had nothing to lose. I moved some living room chairs to form a cozy gathering and sat down on my couch. This felt more than a little strange, but I was intent on giving it an honest try.

"Come now, my family. Let's gather and have a little talk."

I looked up to the ceiling, imagining that was where they'd enter the room.

"Mom, please, sit here. Curt, Dad, come. There's room for everyone."

It was up to me to pull this off—talk to these ghosts, these dead people, my family. As I called the meeting to order, I started to feel something significant was happening.

I soon realized I was going to have to do all the talking; I had no expectations of any dialogue. This would not be a discussion but a monologue, my monologue. They were my captive audience who could not challenge my remarks as they could have done—and often did—when alive. I reached deep inside to unearth the words that would make me win this awful battle. This was my time to break away from the depression caused by the suicides.

"Well, Dad, let's start with you. It's been over six years since you killed yourself. And you know I've worked hard to come to grips with your death, especially your suicide. I remember the time when we were having lunch in the nursing home with Mom. You sat facing an old friend who was in a wheelchair at the next table. He'd lost a lot of ground and sat slumped; his head drooped to the side. I saw you watch him and remember your words: 'I don't *ever* want to live like that.' Then wincing but holding your shaky, eighty-three-year-old composure, you gave me a steely cold stare and said, 'There is no *dignity* in life like that.'

"Dad, I think you made a business decision about your death. You wanted your hard-earned money used for your family's care rather than nursing-home costs. Your suicide was easier to deal with than Curt's because you had lived a long and illustrious life. When you committed suicide, I had Curt as an emotional buffer. But when you checked out, Curt, I was pretty much on my own. Thank God for my friends and therapy."

Then I raised my voice and shouted, "More than anything else, I don't want you dead people poisoning my ability to be happy and at peace. But to get to that, I need to forgive the suicides and expel the demon anger. I refuse to have my future cursed with unfinished business about this."

In Tony Kushner's Pulitzer Prize winning play, *Angels in America*, the ghost of executed Ethel Rosenburg comes to her prosecutor on his deathbed and asks, "Could I *ever* forgive you? I have born my hatred into heaven and made a little star … forgiveness is the hardest thing. It's where love and justice finally meet."

I called up the spirits of my family, embraced them, tangled with them, and chose to spit out the suicides. I'd crossed a threshold.

Or so I thought.

PART III

THE RESULTS

2000 - 2009

Rainforest Breakthrough

Rain is as much a cathartic precipitation as a purveyor of ridiculous sorrows.

—David Guterson, *Our Lady of the Forest*

After Mom's death and the inevitable sorrow, a really Big D came during the summer of 2000. I had the worst depression ever as I felt a fearsome threat to my life. All the shared experiences with my family members were now only in my memory. I knew I had to stop the bad movies in my head so I kept telling myself, *I'm going to hash this out. I will tame it.* After they were all gone, I realized how they had been the hub of my emotional and intellectual life, all my life. We were always there for each other. And everyone read books and newspapers, and we'd talk about politics and conditions in our communities and the world. It was highly stimulating and usually enjoyable.

Simone de Beauvoir, in *She Came to Stay*, describes well my feelings when she wrote of "a harmful mist, a dense vapor … whirling emptiness, the maelstrom … sucking her under … It seemed that in the end she must touch something: peace of mind or despair, something definite; but always she remained … on the brink of emptiness."

All my life, my character had been influenced by my parents and brother. As soon as I was recovering from one veil of grief, another came upon me. Depression permeated my psyche with a vengeance. During the darkest days, I tried chanting a mantra during hour-long brisk walks. "I will grow and develop in new ways because of this loss." I decided I would become someone new.

Several weeks after Mom's death, I had a period of nearly two weeks when I slept between twelve and fifteen hours each night. It was so bizarre that I kept a logbook to see if I could find a pattern or track even the slightest improvement.

Jill called. "How's it going?"

"I'm struggling with the medicine again. I feel sluggish and am sleeping more than I should."

"Oh, dear, Evonne. I'm sorry to hear that you have to fuss with new medicine again. So what's going on now?"

"My shrink put me on some additional meds that have totally zonked me out. For the past two weeks, I've been sleeping twelve to fifteen hours each night."

"Two weeks! Oh, that's awful. Maybe you're coming down with something. Sometimes if the immune system is low, the body tries to restore itself by getting lots of rest."

"No, I feel fine except for the depression. A few days ago, I slept seventeen hours. It's amazing; after all that sleep, I can still sleep the *next* night just as much. It's a double-sided sword—the new medicine has brightened my mood, but if I sleep my life away, what's the use?"

"Oh, Evonne, come on now, this is a phase—adjusting to new meds. You have to give them time for your body to adjust. I admire you, though, because you never give up; you go after it head on."

"Yes, I know. The drowsiness may wear off in time, so it's the old routine of seeing how long I can stick it out with horrible side effects that *may* go away. It bugs the heck out of me. I want solutions, *now*."

"You just have to be patient."

"But even before the new meds, I'd been sleeping lots. Simple things like buying groceries and paying bills seem like big chores. I used to love grocery shopping; now I hate it."

"Hmm. Well that will change. Enjoy what you can. You're doing the right things. It just takes time."

"Thanks, Jill. You're a gem of a friend. I really do appreciate your good head."

I looked at my 2000 travel schedule and realized I had repeated a similar pattern for fifteen years.

Feb. 16–18	Spokane, Washington
March 24–25	Skamania, Washington
April 13–16	Portland, Oregon
April 14–18	Seward, Nebraska
May 3–5	Skamania, Washington
May 12	SeaTac, Washington
May 17–19	Portland, Oregon
May 30–June 5	Providence, Rhode Island
June 15–21	San Francisco, California
July 1–5	Seward, Nebraska
Aug. 2–7	New Orleans, Louisiana
Aug. 13–16	Olympia, Washington
Sept. 13–15	Vancouver, Washington
Oct. 18–20	SeaTac, Washington
Nov. 1–3	Vancouver, British Columbia

At fifty-two, I asked myself, is this how I wanted to spend my next dozen years? Some people thrive on schedules like that. I did for a while. It was stimulating, but there was never enough time to slow down for "moral pondering," as David Guterson says. If I retired, I would have time to read, write, take classes, explore new interests, travel, meet new people, or have a whole new career. The possibilities were unlimited.

Several days later, Jill called. "Just checking up on you. How are you doing?"

"It's still hard to get up in the morning. I hear the alarm; the radio plays for an hour and then shuts off. During that hour, I battle. *Should I get up? I don't want to. Who cares?* I want to avoid everything. I know this will pass. I'm not lazy yet feel guilty and think I should force myself."

"So, can you figure out why this is happening?"

"Well, I think it's a mixed bag: part depression, part meds, and part grieving. It's so weird. Yesterday, I decided to stop the second med the doc gave me two weeks ago—Buspar, for anxiety—yet I still slept until 1 p.m. today. That's another *thirteen-hour* night!"

The next week, I called Jill. "Hi. I have great news. I feel together and up again. What irony—one moment up, one moment down. I'm learning to be more patient and I'm not going to give up trying new meds or whatever it takes to temper this sorrow."

"Oh, Evonne. That's great!"

"I just heard myself say irony, and that smacks of denial. It is ironical, yes, but it's depression, and that's mental illness. How I hate to say that; I don't want to accept that."

"Listen, Evonne, it's not what you call it that counts; it's how you feel and function that's important."

"I guess I've finally resigned myself to the mental illness label, as much as I've fought it. My doc gave me some interesting material about recent research that gave me more understanding. I had a terrible thought when I was feeling super blue recently, something like, 'No wonder Dad and Curt checked out the way they did if they felt as bad as I had and had no psychotherapist or medicine.'"

"But, see … there's a big difference. You're working diligently with your doctor and have such a strong will to find solutions."

"Oh, Jill, you're right, and it's so helpful for me to hear you say that. And, I even feel a twinge of enjoyment in writing coming back. After years of journal writing, I see now how useful it's been in processing my thoughts."

"Well, that's great."

I woke up the next day feeling remarkably better. I believed going off one of my meds was a factor. The excess sleep might go away as my body adjusted and I found the dosage that works best. Sometimes I wanted to throw away all the pills and start from scratch. A possible side effect of my anti-depressant, nefazodone, a generic of Serzone, was that it might cause depression. How nuts was that?

In the pit of sorrow, I knew I had to go deep within to find something that would break the spell. I looked at my schedule and realized it had been nearly eighteen months since I had taken time just for play. I decided a change of pace might help so pushed hard to complete a large work project to spend a few days in the Olympic Rainforest. And it was there, in a rustic cabin, overlooking a pristine lake nestled in pines, where the transformation began. When I arrived, I felt as if my darkness would never lift, the excessive sleep would never cease, and that was just my fate. And then I went hiking.

~ ~ ~

Each time I come to this sacred place, I bow in obeisance to the towering trees. For over twenty-five years, I've been coming here to seek answers. This trip would be no different. The only sounds are the wind and the birds. It's a place where wetness has a smell. I heard the soothing gentle crunch of my well-worn boots connect with the earth as I hiked. How comfortable to be in hiking clothes rather than the suits, nylons, heels, and coordinated jewelry of my working life. This was where I belonged—in the forest—not in hotel conference rooms.

The air in the Olympic Rainforest holds the gentlest rain imaginable. It is so soft you can't even hear the drops, so soft you can't even see the drops, so soft it doesn't even seem like rain. As I hiked, it felt as if microscopic droplets, suspended in air and time, were gently bathing my face. It reminded me of John Muir's description near a Yosemite waterfall, "It is a flood of singing air, water, and sunlight woven into cloth that spirits might wear."

I stopped and studied a clump of trees, twenty or more, whose branches were entwined. They seemed to be a family of the finest kind, embracing and helping each other stand tall. Their limbs were wrapped in moss that was lush, green, and full of life. The shapes were reminiscent of the sensual curves of the human body, though the colors were emerald and olive. In pure silence, these trees had stood alone yet together, undisturbed for hundreds of years. Without their unity, they might not have withstood the storms that have befallen them.

A change began when the misty rain bathed my skin as I hiked. It felt like a cleansing christening, refreshing my body, soul, and mind. It was as if a fever had broken, only this was an evil spell of depression that was lifting as well as the heavy, leaden sleep. They seemed to dissolve like the morning mist. I felt myself break away from fear. I knew I had turned a corner. After a few days hiking, the shadows and darkness gradually dissipated, like the fleeting rays of sun at dusk. I woke up, and it was a new day.

My life now had a direction. I had reached a milestone and moved on. I developed an attitude that the solution was already in progress.

How did I ultimately want to feel? It was an important leap of faith—to trust myself to take me where I needed to go—and resulted in building faith in my intuition.

~ ~ ~

One day out hiking, I spotted a herd of elk. These magnificent giant creatures were racing across an open field at a breathtaking speed. A bull was at the head of a herd, with some sixty elk running behind. Standing tall and proud, he was the leader to whom all paid strict attention, clearly the king, the largest bull with the largest antlers. He darted speedily ahead and returned to beckon the others, like a parade leader, dashing smartly forward, stopping, and turning sprightly to his followers.

As he turned, the herd suddenly stopped, and after a short pause, charged into a circular dance. Not more than a minute later, they stopped and then dashed forward a few hundred feet to begin again the dance. Stopping, twirling, dashing, stopping. It was spring, and there were small calves among them whom the elders were teaching.

After the circle play, all the elk charged at once in a chaotic and random manner, then a pattern gradually emerged, and they were all moving in the same direction again. It was instinctual to them—there was no hesitation or discord. They all knew exactly what to do, and they did it. It was a beautiful, primeval dance—romantic and fetching in its synchronicity.

The word synchronicity was coined by Carl Jung to describe events so timely and moving that they are beyond chance. He referred to synchronicity as, "a vital operating principal in the universe just as real as the laws of physics and the orbits of the planets." He called it a directing intelligence that pushes humans toward psychological and spiritual growth. James Redfield, in *The Celestine Prophecy*, writes about it, "We feel wiser and more capable." The result is that one feels expanded and transformed, able to move toward one's best and most creative self. Redfield calls it an ideal state of functioning, where you increase your sense of well-being and learn things that move your life forward.

My trance from the elk's dance led me to ask, if I wanted to move toward an ideal state of functioning, what would I do? What would it mean? And would it matter? *That's it. I'm going to retire.*

~ ~ ~

When I returned home, I knew I was not the same as when I had left. My need for excessive sleep diminished, and I awoke without that heavy feeling, as though someone had poured molten lead in my body and it had hardened. Those who have felt this frozen immobility of serious depression know what I mean. Proust writes of a similar surge in *Swann's Way*, "A long spell of enforced immobility had stored up an accumulation of vital energy, now felt the need, like a spinning-top wound up and let go, to expand it in every direction."

Somewhere in the midst of the rainforest, my old self had died. I felt I had shed a layer, like a molting snake. I imagined a black shroud of darkness was removed from me. I peered out cautiously, but confidently, into the future. A new self, no longer afraid of depression and suicide was emerging.

At the center of my heart of darkness, my deepest depression, I found a gift, a turning point. I imagined a fork in the road—one path was dark, and the other was where I needed to go to survive. I increased my pace as this view materialized and, without hesitation, turned onto the road of light, to the rest of my life, full of promise. I had learned the most powerful lesson of all, survival, and I was starting a new journey.

After returning to work, I was more focused and productive than I'd been in weeks. I went to bed and got up at reasonable times. I couldn't believe how much better I was—life felt good again. I was enjoying things. I had three days in a row without problems getting up in the morning. There were so many hours in the day now to do things that were neglected during those weeks of heavy sleep. I took pride in being able to perform my job well and put on a good front to my colleagues, even when I was in the worst of it. They hadn't a clue about my ordeals. What joy to feel some simple pleasures of life again.

Hiding depression from co-workers, friends, and even family is common. Many are nearly flawless in this. Kathy Cronkite in *On the Edge of Darkness: Conversations about Conquering Depression*, writes about her skills in camouflage, "My pain was mine alone; my mask of normalcy, almost seamless." The better sleep and focused work turned my head 180 degrees. Shakespeare once called sleep, the "balm of the mind." Cheers, cheers, I was better!

Jill wrote:

> You tickle me so. Talk about full steam ahead—oh, lady, you're doin' it. Even if there's lots of work, you seem enthusiastic. I love your words: Joyous, upbeat, warm, wonderful. It's the beautiful closure of one chapter and on to the next.

If Jill and I weren't in touch for a few weeks, she would call or e-mail two words, "Spill it." That was short for, "What's been going on in your life?" One Saturday morning, the "spill it" call came, and I heard Jill's spirited voice.

"Haven't heard from you for a while—so *spill* it! What's up?"

"I was in Seattle for a few days, putting on my last production managers' conferences, and had some great conversations with people I've worked with for many years. I received warm and wonderful comments as they bid me farewell. It was interesting to be asked about my plans and listen to my answers as I designed my dreams on the fly."

"Oh, yes. Isn't it fun to find out our ideas by hearing ourselves talk with others? The people in our lives are like hundreds of little mirrors reflecting ourselves, aren't they?"

"Oh, Jill, what a beautiful thought."

"How's your mood?"

"My mental health is fine. I felt a twinge of sadness when I arrived home, so doused it with a hike. It's not uncommon for me to feel let down after a conference to which I've devoted so much time and energy. I've come to expect it. It's intense and fun to see the long-planned program, mingle and talk with people, learn new things, and then all that work is suddenly history. But, a good brisk walk usually puts it in perspective."

"Gotta go, lady. Catch ya later."

~ ~ ~

My life was crazy with a zillion details at work, but it would be this way only a few more months. The feeling of letting go was wonderful. What would my life be like when I wouldn't be writing bulletin stories and planning meetings? I had no signs of depression.

Things were great. I continued to feel jazzed. I wondered if I'd ever been as happy as I was now. It was like beginning life all over again. I'd spent two days in Seattle the previous week at a mind-stretching conference. It was a combination of journalists and psychiatrists, my favorite kinds of people. There were also experimental social psychologists, a highly inspiring man, Sheldon Solomon—a professor of psychology at Skidmore College—and a fascinating mix of others from throughout the country who worked with violence issues. Some were writers, reporters, authors; others worked with victims and some with gangs. It was sponsored by the Ernest Becker Foundation in Seattle. (Becker is author of the Pulitzer Prize winning *The Denial of Death* and *Escape from Evil*.) The foundation conducts programs and supports research on how Becker's ideas can be applied to effect positive change. It was fascinating, and I came home eager to learn more.

I told my shrink that before, nothing was interesting, and now I felt like the old journalist, and everything was interesting.

One powerful speaker was a psychiatrist who worked with people who had lost loved ones in violent deaths. I immediately thought of murder and physical abuse. Then he included suicide as a violent death, and I felt as though I'd been hit by a load of bricks. It jarred me as, heretofore, I'd not thought of either my father's or brother's suicide as violent. There were no guns, knives, or blood … instead, car exhaust and aspirin. His point was that *all* suicides are violent. It was profound and enlightening but rather than stirring up pain, it made me feel I'd made a difficult and powerful journey. I left with positive and meaningful attitudes about life and death. Becker would have been proud.

As I looked toward retirement, I realized that if I was ever to write the book that had been evolving in my head for years, now was the time. To help the process, I read Sam Keen's *The Sacred Journey, Your Quest for Life's Higher Meaning* and found some powerful questions: "What battles have you fought? Who have been your helpers, your mentors? What's important? What's not important? What illusions have you lost? What longings are still there? What hasn't happened for you yet?"

Around that time, I had a dramatic dream about escaping a storm. I was fearlessly climbing up a rope ladder, even though I knew it would be scary and difficult. Behind me was a cute little girl with beautiful, bouncing blond curls tied with pretty ribbons. She was about six years old, full of smiles, and followed me closely. I soon realized this girl was me. She was having the time of her life, and it was enormously comforting to have her with me. The sunny blue skies suddenly changed to a somber and menacing gray, and a brutal rainstorm came upon us. I was seriously frightened and didn't think we'd survive. Lightning flashed, thunder roared, and a strong wind blew me off the ladder into the stormy sea below. I was horribly frightened, and the little golden-haired girl was nowhere in sight. Then I saw something like a battered, miniature Noah's ark—a crude wooden boat floating in the water. I climbed aboard, paddled furiously, and transformed the boat into a sophisticated hydroplane. I was able to pull the machine into the air. As I sat at the controls, it reminded me of flying Dad's Cessna 172 back when I was in college. I pulled the stick forward, and the nose moved up from the water, into the sky, and away from the storm. It was an arduous battle, but I used my skills and escaped the danger.

A few weeks into my retirement, I wrote:

> I see it in the mirror. There's a new aliveness in my face. It shows most in my eyes. I can't remember ever feeling this peaceful and content. Could this be? Could I feel this happy? Is this what life will be like now that so many responsibilities are gone?

It was a cold and wet January morning in 2001, and I was on the familiar road to my psychiatrist's office. It had been three months since I'd seen him and was making one final visit to wrap things up. My thick brown hair bounced as I strutted up the stairs to say farewell to the man who had been an anchor to me through the darkest days of my life.

I was buried in work when I had last visited, but that seemed light-years away now. My psychotherapy had helped me develop the courage, which led me to the dramatic decision to retire and write this book. I had a booming desire to get on with my life and felt no need to continue therapy. I felt strong, proud, and a little smug. I remembered reciting lines to Dr. Peterson from "Amazing Grace" some time ago, "Through many dangers, toils and snares, we have already come."

The song in my head was interrupted when Dr. Peterson opened the door to his waiting room. After I settled into my familiar chair in his familiar office, I quickly whistled through how my life was so grand. And then I became serious.

"A crucial part of my therapy, I believe, has been my ability to finally differentiate myself from my brother and father. I've thought about the many differences between us and realized I'm not them. They were individuals, and so am I. I don't carry the physical or emotional pain they did, and there's nothing to say that I can't be different. The reasons they took their lives were idiosyncratic to them—separate cases with different motivations. Dad was an old man and headed for the nursing home. Curt's death meant the end of two decades of suffering. I have none of those conditions."

"That's right. Good."

"Another way I differentiated myself from their suicides—and this is significant—is that neither of them had the experiences with suicides that I've had. I've worked to establish a sharp distinction, a deep and solid line between them and me."

Then I bounced back into my dreamy retirement mode and described as reality so many things that before I'd talked about as longings—reading, writing, exercising, going to lectures, book readings, the theater, and symphony.

"I'm now free from the shackles of thirty years of deadlines, schedules, and responsibilities. I'm pruning old views of myself and planting seeds for new growth. I've integrated the lessons of the past into a more evolved person."

In the last minutes of my final fifty-minute hour, I challenged Peterson for a summary statement. *Lots of luck*, I thought, *in boiling down my years of therapy into a few sentences.*

The man of few words replied, "It seems as though your life is in a renaissance."

I felt all the muscles in my face crinkle up in joy as I nodded in agreement, stood up, and said goodbye. As I drove away, I realized it was hard to bid farewell to someone who had played such a significant role in my life. Week by week, for years, I had deliberated my life with him. The more I worked in therapy, the more I freed the shackles that slowed my positive perspective.

I got in my car, and as I stepped on the accelerator, my psyche powered up, too. *I don't need you anymore,* I thought as I nodded in the direction of Peterson. *Everyone's dead, and I've never felt so peaceful and happy.*

I wondered what adventures lay ahead.

SIXTEEN WORDS FOR WATER

We do not see things as they are. We see things as we are.

—Anais Nin

It was a dark January morning, and I was reading my newspapers when I saw a photo that took my breath away. It was a picture of my brother. My heart almost stopped. Curt had been dead for nearly three years. Why would his picture be in the paper? I was spooked. I stared at the image and read the caption.

Oh, it's not Curt, of course not. It was a character in a play—a play about Ezra Pound. I knew immediately that I must see this play. I needed to see this actor, who—in the newspaper photo—looked exactly like Curt.

In the days ahead, I was preoccupied with anticipation. Ezra Pound, ah yes, that rascally American poet. It struck me that this play, *Sixteen Words for Water*, by Billy Marshall Stoneking, would be strange because, not only did this actor look like Curt, but there were also parallels in the lives of Curt and Pound. Both had been locked in psychiatric hospitals against their wills. Both had acerbic wit and a powerful command of language. Both fervently defended their beliefs. And now, this actor was an exact visual duplicate of Curt.

According to the review, "During World War II, [Pound's] radio broadcasts from Rome which [he] said were to defend the [U.S.] Constitution, outraged the sensibilities of the Western world. He was arrested by the U.S. government, charged with treason and jailed. His lawyers advised he plead insanity to avoid execution. The next year he was acquitted, but declared mentally ill and committed to a mental hospital. After thirteen years of continuous appeals from writers for his release, he was judged incurably insane and freed in 1958."

The evening finally arrived and I decided to doll up a bit. I pulled a pretty dress from my closet and my best winter coat—it had been Mom's—the Pierre Cardin black wool with the velvet collar. I drove the thirty-five miles to Olympia, expecting an unusual evening. The State Theater was a new place for me, and the ambiance was appealing—old and cozy with character. As the play was about to begin, a young man announced the actors would be available for questions following the show. *Oh great, I'll be able to see the actor playing Pound up close.*

Both photos above are Curt Mead. The photo on the left is Jim Fulkerson, the actor who played Ezra Pound in the play. Reprinted with permission from Harlequin Productions.

The lights dimmed, and a gentle spotlight illuminated a man on stage in disheveled clothes, hunched over an old typewriter, apparently sleeping, and obviously Pound. Hanging above the cluttered room was a labyrinth canopy made from string, full of papers, attached with clothespins. Pulleys allowed the raising and lowering of the web in Pound's room in the mental hospital.

A door opened, and a woman with a briefcase entered. Pound awakened and stood, and I gasped. I knew he was an actor, but he was Curt incarnate. It was inconceivable! The man on stage was my brother's identical twin. There was no way I could have prepared for this extraordinary experience. I knew this wasn't Curt—that would be ludicrous—but what was going on? Why this live rendition of him three years after his death? Why is this happening?

I survived the double whammy of two family suicides, seven years since Dad's and three years since Curt's; those beasts were tamed. It had been months since my dream of their suicides chasing me in the form of anthropomorphic tanks. What fate caused this churning of memories, this manifestation of Curt? I tried to focus on the actor, to absorb all I could from this bizarre experience, watching a mirror image of my dead brother walk and talk.

I found myself taking on the persona of the woman in the play who talked with Curt/Pound. She was crisp and forthright and tried hard to keep the upper hand when Curt/Pound raved about subjects that rankled him. I remembered times like that with Curt. Echoes of conversations with him during his manic raves poured into my head when she said:

> You know, I think you like it here. The noble victim. The abused visionary. The genius in the madhouse ... You think you're so smart, don't you? ... You still think you know more than everyone else. The poor, misunderstood genius. The helpless victim who believes he has all the answers if only the world will listen to him.

It wasn't Pound and a woman on stage, it was Curt and I. But no, this was a play! What was going on down there was not real. That wasn't my brother; that was an actor. I was not on that stage, I was sitting in a theater. *Come on, get real.*

From the time of Curt's committal to his death twenty years later, he never faltered in his conviction that he had been framed and hospitalized because certain people didn't like his ideas and wanted to get him out of the political scene. He was, like Pound, the "abused visionary," the "misunderstood genius."

In Pound's room were some drawings of cave paintings, human-like creatures who had no mouths, the Wandjina—the supreme spirit being of Aboriginal natives. Pound held up a drawing, and the dialogue went like this:

Betsy: There are several hundred of them in the caves of
           Australia.
Pound: So, what happened to the mouths?
Betsy: They weren't needed any more.
Pound: Weren't needed?
Betsy: The Aborigines believe the Wandjina created the entire
           world, with words, with names. All they had to do was
           name something and it would exist. Trees, mountains,
           animals. Everything. They say if the Wandjina hadn't
           been stopped they would've made too many things.
           So the mouths were taken away.
Pound: Taken away?
Betsy: Removed. To stop the names.
Pound: To stop them speaking.
Betsy: If they'd kept going, they would've destroyed the world.
           There would've been too many things.
Pound: The difference between the Wandjina and me is that it
           was the *gods* who took their mouths away ... *mine* was
           removed by the State.

I groaned. This was exactly like Curt, talking about his fall from power, how he'd been silenced at the height of his career and wrongfully committed to a psyche ward. The play was about to end when the action on stage was halted by a maniacal and piercing scream offstage. It reminded everyone that the setting was a mental hospital. While the play continued, I was mentally absent. That scream. Something happened inside me, like a bolt of lightning—that scream stirred up a memory I'd buried for twenty years.

It was the day after Curt's committal, and Dad and I were allowed to visit him. We were escorted through locked doors and found Curt in a room, reading a book. His brow was furrowed, and he looked as stressed and angry as I'd ever seen him. He glared at us with horror and disillusionment. We made some small talk when our exchange, like the one in the play, was halted by a piercing, maniacal scream down the hall.

Curt snarled at us, "Now, isn't this going to be a nice place for me to stay?"

While my mind was in that memory, the play ended, and the audience was invited to the post-play discussion. I slowly broke from my trance and moved near the front to see Curt/Pound up close. I wanted to ask him a question. The actors sat on the edge of the stage, and I stared at the man who played Pound. He didn't have a clue about my psychic baggage; to him, I was simply an admiring fan. A handsome gentleman in a charcoal turtleneck and tweed jacket stepped forward.

"Good evening. My name is Matt White, and I'm the director of the play. Thank you for coming. So, questions? Anyone?"

A woman in the back asked, "How do you resolve the conflict between Pound, the brilliant poet, writer, and defender of free speech, and Pound, the fascist, anti-Semitic bigot?"

The director responded, "On one hand, there is no reason to resolve the conflict. Resolving conflict is for Hollywood—nice tidy packages. In this play, *we* must become resolved to the fact that this human being is capable of all these qualities and more.

"On the other hand, it's important to understand that not everything Pound (or anyone else) says is what he means. As he says in the play, 'What comes out of the mouth doesn't necessarily explain anything.' Was Pound *really* anti-Semitic? He had numerous close friends who were Jewish. He hated banks, capitalism, and what had been done to pervert the political theories of Jefferson and Adams."

The director glanced at his watch, "We'll take two more questions." My hand flew up.

"Yes, over there."

Oh dear, I might miss my chance.

A deep baritone voice bellowed out, "What are some of the lines you found the most memorable?" The actor stepped forward and, after a brief statement, fell into the character of Pound: "The worst treason is the one we commit against ourselves—speaking when we should be silent; or worse, being silent when we should speak … Those who can still *see* and speak *must* make themselves heard."

"Last question?"

My hand flew up again.

"Yes, here in front."

I turned toward Curt's apparition and took a deep breath. "What did you learn about Pound, by crawling into his skin and memorizing your lines, that might not be apparent to someone seeing the play for the first time?"

There he was, staring into my eyes, talking to me, but I had no idea what he was saying because all I could think of was how much he looked exactly like Curt. My first thought was how odd that he didn't recognize me as his sister, but to him I was just a face in the crowd. Then I tuned in his words, something about the "troubling character of Pound, reminiscent of Willy Loman in *Death of a Salesman.*"

He looked me squarely in the eye and continued, "It was as if Pound was passionate to a fault, if there is such a thing. He was void of tolerance with any position counter to his and patient and demonstrative with those wearing his same cloak."

Passionate to a fault—sounded like Curt. Maybe if he wouldn't have been so damned passionate, he would still be alive.

The discussion was over, and I wanted to run up and hug this man and have him really be Curt and have all that suicide mess be just another bad dream. What if I could have my brother back and we could sit down and talk? But I didn't go to the actor; I couldn't—it would be too strange. How could I possibly explain his effect on me? The evening had been bizarre enough.

As I drove home, I felt more of the pain of Curt's suicide dissolve. The windshield wipers seemed to sweep away not only rain but also the haunting power of Curt's death. There was a further distancing, another milestone in my healing. Curt changed from my brother whom I'd been mourning to more like a character in a play.

In *Swann's Way*, Marcel Proust describes a time like this as "one of those days which are not like other days, on which time starts afresh, casting aside the heritage of the past, declining its legacy of sorrows."

Several years later, I was at a theater in another town and, as I settled into my seat and read the program, realized that the Pound actor was in the play I was about to see. When he appeared on the stage, he bore no resemblance to my brother, whatsoever. During the intermission, I found large photos of the actors on display in the foyer, and in this view, as well, the actor looked nothing like Curt. And I was glad.

Coming Alive

I read and write and things I have never understood become clear.

—Annie Dillard, *Pilgrim at Tinker Creek*

I t was the first spring of my retirement, and I picked up a copy of the *Northwest Dharma News* because I wanted to learn more about Buddhism and meditation. I read about a place called Cloud Mountain that offered retreats near Vader, about seventy miles south of Tacoma. I enrolled in one called, "Women and Writing," taught by renowned Buddhist author and scholar, Sandy Boucher.

Part of our work involved writing about the four elements: fire, water, air, and earth. About fire, I wrote:

> How does it feel to have finally begun to come live again? How does it feel to have finally begun my life-long dream of writing a book? I courageously pulled from my closet the thick stacks of papers, notebooks, and folders that held family letters and my journals spanning thirty years. It was my conscious and satisfying choice to try to evoke some of the beautiful, intense, and tragic experiences of my life. I want to express the moments that changed me forever. I'm doing this for my son's understanding and for my own enlightenment—this attempt to synthesize the lessons I've learned. I have a deep yearning to resolve my lingering anguish and transform it to equanimity and understanding.

About the element earth, I wrote:

> Pt. Defiance Park is one of the largest city parks in the country, and I call it my mental health park. For nearly two decades, I've

been sorting out my life on its twenty-seven miles of old growth forest trails. Sadness, confusion, anger, and frustration have all been tempered and tamed during my time here. Heavy burdens gradually lighten, then nearly dissolve, as the melancholy toxins that haunt me are neutralized.

If this tree can endure, thrive, and bring peace and beauty into the world for five hundred years, I can grow and thrive, too. The serenity and grace of the towering pines are there for me to model and absorb. The trees have grown strong by the storms that have pushed them to near destruction, just as I have been made strong by the storms in my life.

And now there is peace in the forest—my forest. So much water of sadness has flowed through the streams that my bedrock glistens in the sun. Sparkles of light are reflected in nearly every part of my life. Peace and serenity fill my spirit.

~ ~ ~

While the writing exercises were worthwhile, little did I know how my introduction to Kwan Yin, the centuries-old Buddhist goddess of compassion, would affect my future in a profound way.

Boucher described an experience as a young woman when she was in Kansas City and saw the larger-than-life, painted wooden statue of Kwan Yin at the Nelson-Atkins Museum of Art. That happenstance launched her life-long study of this goddess. Boucher wrote *Discovering Kwan Yin, Buddhist Goddess of Compassion* and has published four other books on Buddhism. Attending several of her retreats significantly broadened my understanding of Buddhism, Kwan Yin, meditation and writing. In my study, I found many names for Kwan Yin:

Avalokitesvara
Gom Lin (Thailand)
Guan Shih Yin (China)
Guanyin of the Southern Sea
Gwan Shr Yin
Kanin (Bali)
Kannon or Kanzeon (Japan)
Kwan Seum Bosal (Korea)
Kwannon-sama
Quan Am (Vietnam)

Quan Yin
Ta pei Kuan Yin
Water Moon Kwan Yin

It is not incidental to my story that when I first saw the statue she had the Water Moon label, and that's what I've called her ever since.

The earliest depictions of her were in the form of a male deity, Avalokitesvara, but by the twelfth century, in China, she had evolved into a female. She is sometimes depicted with a thousand arms and a thousand eyes, which help her find and aid all who beckon her. The Bodhisattva (an enlightened being) is especially called upon by those in distress or danger, and there are many legends about the miracles she's performed.

Boucher passed around a postcard of the statue and suggested that if we ever visit Kansas City, we should see it. I tucked the thought away as I visit a friend in Kansas City every few years. I held the postcard a long time and stared at the vibrant orange of her garment. It was so striking.

When I returned home, there was a letter in my mail that the Seward Airport Authority would be honoring my father, among other founding members, at an event the next week in Nebraska. Dad had been dead for seven years, so this was not something I was expecting. I quickly decided I wanted to be there, that it would be good to visit old friends in Seward and my friend in Kansas.

The next week, when I saw the breathtaking statue, I was awed and immensely calmed. Though seated, she is nearly eight feet tall and more than five feet wide. When I walked into the Chinese Temple Gallery where she resides, I spotted a docent and introduced myself. The woman told me that Thomas Hoving, director of the Metropolitan Museum in New York City for many years (1967–1977), was once asked to identify the thirty most outstanding pieces of art in the world, and he included this statue of Kwan Yin.

"How old is the statue?"

"We guess about one thousand years. She was carved sometime during the eleventh and twelfth centuries during the Liao Dynasty from 907–1125 or the Jin Dynasty from 1115–1234."

"How did this statue from China happen to land in Kansas City?"

"In 1903, Langdon Warner, a scholar of Asian art at Harvard, was retained by the Nelson-Atkins to purchase Chinese art. Warner contacted his prize student, Lawrence Sickman, who was on a fellowship in China, to assist him, and it was Sickman who found the statue. Sickman eventually became director of the Nelson-Atkins in 1953, though his involvement with the museum began some twenty years earlier."

"How interesting. And who were Nelson and Atkins?"

"William Rockhill Nelson was a Kansas City newspaperman in the early 1900s, and Mary Atkins was a school teacher and a wealthy widow of a real estate speculator. Their separate estates each provided for a museum, but those involved brought the two estates together to create one, magnificent museum."

When we finished talking, I sat near the statue with her bright orange garb and, for a long time, meditated in the quiet majesty of this powerful icon.

RUTTGER'S ROBIN

I pray to the birds because I believe they will carry the messages of my heart upward. I pray to them because I believe in their existence, the way their songs begin and end each day—the invocations and benedictions of Earth.

—Terry Tempest Williams, *Refuge*

During Mom's eight years in the nursing home, most of my vacation time was spent visiting her in Nebraska. After she died, I knew I'd finally have time to visit Minnesota. When I booked my flight in the spring of 2002, I realized I'd be in Minnesota on May 1, the fourth anniversary of Curt's death. *That's fine*, I thought. *I'll be visiting friends and relatives and distracted from thinking about him. Besides, this is easier now that a few years have passed.* Several weeks later, I was checking into Ruttger's Bay Lake Lodge near Aitkin, a lovely place I'd visited many times as a child with my family.

"That's for three nights, right?" the lady asked. "April 29, 30, and May 1?"

When I heard "May 1" aloud, my mind jumped to Curt. "Oh, yes," I finally said.

When May 1 came, I awoke and gazed out my window on the serenity of the gently rippling Bay Lake. This was one of many Minnesota lakes where Curt and I swam together as children. It was wonderful to have this peace about him. I spent the rest of the day visiting friends and thought no more of him until returning that evening. It came to me. Yes, that's how it should be, a little touching moment of remembrance and, then, on with life. I basked in my spiritual evolution.

The next morning, after checking out, I moved toward the door, and the young lady who had helped me stepped in the same direction.

Once outside, she pointed across the way and said, "Did you see the robin that made a nest over there?"

"No. Oh my, how peaceful she looks."

The morning sun warmed our faces, and we stopped to watch the mamma bird sit motionless in her nest, entirely absorbed in her task of making a new life. I remembered the dead bird on the driveway when Curt died. And now, on the anniversary of his death, near a lake in Minnesota where we shared childhood play, came this robin to start a new life.

~ ~ ~

Two months later, on a pristine day in July, I rose early to drive to Mount Rainier for a day of hiking. It had been four years since the dead bird on the driveway at Curt's death and two years since the dead bird in my living room after Mom's death. The scenes were vivid, and I knew they would be in my book; I wanted to write them but wasn't sure how. I sensed the tone and approach ripening but didn't push it or worry, knowing it would eventually be clear.

The anticipation of enjoying Mount Rainier inspired me to try to move ahead with the bird stories, which had been flying around in my head for a long time. I wanted to get them corralled into words on paper. I brought my handheld tape recorder, and as I drove to the mountain, I talked the bird stories out loud as if I was telling them to a friend. It worked great, and I was certain I had some good first drafts. I was surprised how relieved I felt after I'd spoken them, as if a scab had fallen from a wound. Remembering those times was emotional, so I thought I'd put the bird stories aside for a while … until I went to my mailbox the next day.

There was a newsletter from Ruttger's Bay Lake Lodge where I'd stayed a couple of months ago. I glanced at the front page and was startled to see a photograph of the robin's nest I had seen on the anniversary of Curt's death and a story about what I had seen. They'd named the robin Ruby after Ruby Treloar, who was a long-time resort employee and had been a family friend for years.

The day before, I had poured out my heart into a tape recorder about the dead robin on the driveway when Curt died, and today, I

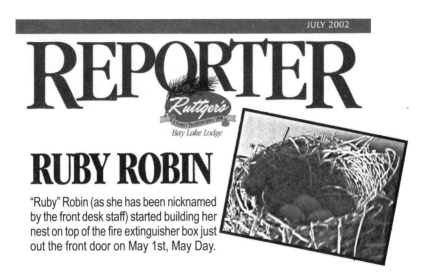

JULY 2002

REPORTER

Ruttger's
A FAMILY TRADITION SINCE 1898
Bay Lake Lodge

RUBY ROBIN

"Ruby" Robin (as she has been nicknamed by the front desk staff) started building her nest on top of the fire extinguisher box just out the front door on May 1st, May Day.

read about the impending birth of a new robin in the nest I saw on the anniversary of his death.

I recalled the lady at the reception desk who had made a point of showing me the nest. Was it coincidental that a robin came to Ruttger's to build this nest when I was there? Was it coincidental the lady pointed this out to me? Was it coincidental that Ruttger's printed a story and photo about the robin? Was it coincidental that I focused intently on those story drafts the day before the newsletter arrived?

Perhaps it's silly, but I see birds differently now. I'll be in my kitchen and see them swoop onto my deck. Sometimes they perch near the window, point their beady little eyes directly inside, and watch me. I greet them, bless them, thank them for stopping by, and then they flutter away.

I work hard now to become more observant of everything around me. I want to be sure not to miss any messages.

~ ~ ~

The next summer, I was sleeping soundly in my mesh-roofed tent overlooking Puget Sound when I suddenly awoke in a state of peak awareness. Though alone, I felt a comforting presence of someone, as if a spiritual power surrounded me. I felt focused with an uncommon awareness and sensibility. Then I saw a huge, vibrant orange ball on the horizon where the water met the dark sky. I was puzzled. What was that bright ball that appeared so suddenly in the night? I'd never seen anything like it. Then I realized I was witnessing a moonset.

It was powerful and jarred me in a deep and positive way. Though I couldn't put words around it, I knew something had happened—there was some message or meaning. It wasn't just another beautiful slice of nature I had witnessed. What was the power of watching that giant orange ball slip into the sea? Little did I know that it would be years before the true meaning of the experience would be clear.

There was really a lot more to it than a simple moonset.

MODELS FOR HAPPINESS

[There are] a few great artists who do us the service, when they awaken in us ... what richness, what variety lies hidden, unknown to us, in that vast, unfathomed and forbidding night of our soul.

—Marcel Proust, *Swann's Way*

I felt a huge loss of intellectual stimulation after my parents and brother died. As my heroes fell, I needed new mentors and found many in books. The extent of my changes would not have been possible without the many authors who enriched my sensibilities. Retirement brought me more time for reading that provided positive insights.

A friend recommended a book by Simone de Beauvoir. As I read her and grew to know her, I felt a special attachment because she helped advance the positive changes in my temperament and a balancing of my heart. I was not alone with my mix of sorrow and joy. Hardly. There were others, like Beauvoir, who had forged great happiness from periods of unthinkable sorrow. I became a serious student of Beauvoir and read twenty-five books by or about her. I hadn't planned this but found myself attracted to her and latched onto her as a vibrant new role model. Learning about Beauvoir's "spirited need" (Catharine Savage Brosman, *Simone de Beauvoir Revisited*) to identify and scrutinize the elements that shaped her destiny helped me believe I was on the right track. Beauvoir had a "feverish will to live" which I came to cherish. When I read about Beauvoir's "ardent desire" to express both the horror and joy of existence, my own writing was fueled. Beauvoir and others served as life rafts to me as I tried to conquer the suicide beasts and depression. I slowly created my new psyche—one that would not be haunted by suicide.

Beauvoir describes how writing is a way to forge an indelible portrait of your life, "like mounted insects, as permanent judgments." I realized the book I would write would become my permanent memory of events, and therefore, how crucial it was to be clear and correct. Every word had to be true—100-percent pure of embellishment.

I wanted to move from sadness to a life of happiness. But how? In Beauvoir's novel, *The Mandarins*, Anne Dubreuilh became a psychiatrist because she wanted "to help people … rid themselves of the obstacles they place in the way of their happiness."

While I didn't put the suicide beasts in my path, I knew I was the only one who could push them aside. When I needed courage, I thought of how strongly Beauvoir modeled those qualities under circumstances significantly more dire than mine. Growing up in Paris during World War I, she witnessed bombings, blackouts, and food shortages. She was in her thirties during World War II and writes memorably of the hardships living under Nazi occupation for four years.

My relatives and friends were not murdered or tortured in war. My husband was not a POW. I didn't have to scrounge the garbage for rotten meat to survive. She was profoundly saddened by the horrors but transformed that trauma into happiness. Trauma into happiness? If guns can be turned into plowshares, why not trauma into happiness? Beauvoir "built her happiness on firm ground and beneath immutable constellations," writes Carol Ascher in *Simone de Beauvoir: A Life of Freedom*. What a smart approach and worthy of emulation. Firm ground? Immutable constellations? Where could I find these? Could I build them? What could be my immutable constellations?

I realized my aim of internal peace couldn't be forced but had to come naturally. Nonetheless, I thought of the happiest times of my life and seized the images and words of those events to inspire me in my darkest hours.

"[Beauvoir] built herself an internal citadel where anything that might disturb her happiness was rejected," according to biographers Claude Francis and Fernande Gontier. Oh yes. Me, too. That's what I wanted, but how could I build an internal citadel? What was this core of armor that prevented the intrusion of thoughts that might disturb happiness? I'd had great moments of happiness, but they faded. People change, move, or die. What then of happiness? Must it be relinquished only to memory?

My happiness needed to have its *deepest* anchors outside people and external things, which is to say, internal. Similar ideas have been proclaimed for thousands of years. In the *Tao Te Ching* you'll find, "If you look to others for fulfillment, you will never truly be fulfilled." And in *The Charge of the Goddess*, "If that which you seek you do not find within, you will never find it without."

I was inspired by these rich ideas that fed my soul.

~ ~ ~

My phone rang, and the cheerful lady chirped, "Spill it!"

"Hey, Jill. Hi."

"So what have you been up to?"

"I saw a fascinating play in Seattle last week that really stirred me up."

"What was it?"

"Luigi Pirandello's *Six Characters in Search of an Author*."

"Oh, Pirandello! Yes, he's quite an interesting man. Didn't he win the Nobel Prize for literature once?"

"Yes. I just read it in the program—1934."

"So what stirred you up?"

"Well, it made me think about times in my life when I felt like an unrealized character, incomplete in some way, with restless longing for new experiences. I remember that feeling when I decided to leave Aitkin—that my life wasn't quite what I wanted yet, that I needed to find new challenges. It made me think about the power of the mind over the body and the impact of choice. It made me realize that I'm not trapped inside a script, unlike the characters in the play. I'm the playwright of my life."

"Well, to a certain extent."

"Sure. Another insight the play brought was that as our experiences change, so do our illusions. It reminded me of those great lines from Joseph Conrad in his essay, *Youth*, where he describes the romance of illusions. I first read it in college, and the tattered paperback has stayed with me ever since. Every few years, I pull it out and re-read it. I have it right here. Do you have a minute? May I read it to you?"

"Sure."

"Okay. Here goes:

> By all that's wonderful it is the sea, I believe, the sea itself—
> or is it youth alone? Who can tell? But you here—you all had
> something out of life: money, love—whatever one gets on
> shore—and, tell me, wasn't that the best time, that time when
> we were young at sea …
>
> And we all nodded at him: the man of finance, the man of
> accounts, the man of law, we all nodded at him over the polished
> table that like a still sheet of brown water reflected our faces, lined,
> wrinkled; our faces marked by toil, by deceptions, by success,
> by love; our weary eyes looking still, looking always, looking
> anxiously for something out of life, that while it is expected is
> already gone—has passed unseen, in a sight, in a flash—together
> with youth, with the strength, with the romance of illusions.

"Oh, yes. That's beautiful. I see why you like it."

"So, my mellowing maturity gives me fresh eyes to see life as a continuum where there's always opportunity for change. No matter how old or ingrained we become, there are still unfinished tasks, untraveled roads, unread books."

"So the theme of the play was something like reality vs. illusion?"

"I think that would be fair. It reminded me of my struggle to believe Curt's wild stories and getting caught up in his conspiracy theories about his commitment to the psyche ward. It's a good question—what's real and what isn't?"

"Yes, and how do people decide who is mad and who is sane? It's a fine line."

"Absolutely. In the play, the characters are trapped, and because they have no script, they're unrealized. They want an author to give them voices so they can change, much as we look to relationships, literature, and art to satisfy our needs to live realized lives."

"Oh, how interesting."

"It also made me think about how our illusions change. One of the characters in the play tells the others … let me grab my notes. He tells the others "not to count too heavily on reality as you feel it today, since, like that of yesterday, it may prove an illusion for you tomorrow."

"So the actors made you feel as though life is really a slippery slope and you never know what's going to happen?"

"Yes. Pirandello asks the characters to "think of all those illusions that mean nothing to you now … This present reality … is fated to seem a mere illusion to you tomorrow.""

"Well, hey! I gotta go. We'll check on those tomorrows another day."

"You bet!"

I read more and learned that three main themes pervade most of Pirandello's work: truth, identity, and mental illness. One of his characters asks, "What would it be like to be stuck in a play … in a reality [that] can't change?" The irony is that in many ways, we are stuck in a reality that cannot change.

Pirandello's character admits that his reality is immutable but proclaims that reality for real people is "a transitory and fleeting illusion." That's not especially settling until we feel comfortable enough to jump into the fluidity of life and accept the good and the bad with grace, that good old, sweet-sounding "Amazing Grace." Pirandello believed our illusions change according to our will and sentiments, appearing "today in one manner and tomorrow who knows how?"

~ ~ ~

Jill called. "Hi there, lady. So what have you been up to?"

"Well, I went to the library and got a book with the text of the play, and after reading it, some more thoughts were churned up. I'm calling this my lessons from Luigi."

"So, why is this all so important to you?"

"It's making me think a lot about *my* character realization and times when I felt like an unrealized character. One time was when I'd reached a pinnacle, graduating from college in 1970. Completing this life-long dream, I came to realize my unrealized character. I was twenty-two, and my life was on the launching pad.

"Another time I felt like an unrealized character was when my husband and I left Seward. We had been successful publishers of my dad's weekly paper for three years but, at age twenty-seven, wanted to test our wings in a larger world. After the constant deadlines, I reveled in the excitement of serendipity. We challenged ourselves in ways we wouldn't have by staying in our familiar routine. We allowed ourselves soul-searching time to look at new opportunities.

"Another time I felt unrealized was when I was working at a weekly newspaper in Portland, Oregon. I wanted to be like Woodward and Bernstein and instead had to write a story about fake fingernails."

"Oh, yes, I remember you telling me about that."

"I was thirty and knew I'd find a better place in the world."

"Hey, listen. I'm going to the symphony tonight, so gotta run. Later, lady."

Beauvoir critic Elaine Marks writes in her *Critical Essays on Simone de Beauvoir*, "The molting of illusion is a repeated experience." I pondered her idea and concluded that we shed illusions when our experiences teach us they are no longer valid. Like a molting snake, we replace our illusions with new ones that we think are true at the time.

~ ~ ~

Books have opened my heart and mind resulting in life-changing thoughts and actions. Salman Rushdie described clearly what happened between me and Simone de Beauvoir and other authors. Rushdie wrote, "When a reader falls in love with a book, it leaves its essence inside him, like radioactive fallout in an arable field, and after that there are certain crops that will no longer grow in him, while other, stranger, more fantastic growths may occasionally be produced."

I was in a time of significant growth, sifting through ideas learned from reading, seeing the play with a character who looked and acted like Curt and experiencing my first public book reading. After years of focusing on subjects related to newspaper work, a most pleasurable leap into retirement was reading books on a range of other subjects. For years, I'd collected titles recommended to me from a variety of colleagues, written on cocktail napkins, hotel notepads, and ripped bits of paper. I added many myself about writing, depression, and mental illness. During my first year of retirement, I read forty-two books.

Each book provided new ideas, insights, and awakenings. In 2000, my last year at work, and 2001, my first year of retirement, I kept lists of the books I read. (See Appendix.)

~ ~ ~

On a bright sunny day with a cloudless blue sky, I was transfixed by the beauty of a glacial lake in the Olympics and saw one of Mother Nature's magic tricks—disappearing birds. About a dozen birds were flying in synchrony above the lake, and their images were mirrored in the still water. I turned my head for a moment, and when I looked back, the birds were gone. What happened to them? Then they reappeared, which is to say, I saw them again. Of course, those silly birds didn't dissolve. They simply turned in a way that the sun made them invisible to me. It made me realize that surely, the dimensions of the universe are far beyond what we mortals see. Longfellow knew this when he wrote, "The sky is filled with stars, invisible by day."

Another time, on the bank of an Olympic Peninsula lake, the sun blessed me with its warmth. The reflection on the water of the wooded hillside on the opposite shore resembled long, tightly woven dreadlocks in hues of olive and blue-gray. It was a dance of the wind, water, and retreating sun. The shapes and colors changed as they quivered from a gentle breeze. It's how Proust described the water lilies on Guermantes Way "ceaselessly changing yet remaining always in harmony ... with all that is most profound, most evanescent, most mysterious."

Oh, I believe in the magic of the rainforest, the mysteries of nature, and the miracles of life. The images of the dreadlocks on the water did not really fade—it was only my vision of them that changed.

COMMON TO COUNTLESS

Come to the edge. We might fall. Come to the edge. It's too high! Come to the edge. And they came, and we pushed. And they flew.

—Christopher Logue, *Come to the Edge*

When I was mired in depression, I found hope in the words of a bona fide depression expert, Andrew Solomon, "People who have been through a depression and are stabilized often have a heightened awareness of the joyfulness of everyday existence." I reveled in those thoughts, and coming to that awareness was a positive jog in my journey.

In Solomon's 2002 Pulitzer Prize winning book, *The Noonday Demon: An Atlas of Depression,* he writes, "When you've been depressed, you lose some of your fear of crisis." I found that comforting, too. If tragic events come my way again, I'll have armor and thick skin.

Katherine Graham writes in her Pulitzer Prize winning memoir, *Personal History,* about the benefits of talking with her friend Warren Buffet. "I heard myself talk when I was with him, and I always got a better idea of what I was saying."

That's what my years of psychotherapy were like. In retrospect, I see that I was continually improving my mental health—though it seemed more often than not a bumpy road. One time, after months of weekly sessions, I thought my life was going well and considered discontinuing. However, after that fifty-minute hour, I ended up saying things that amounted to significant breakthroughs. Had I not been in therapy, I likely would not have said those things to myself (or anyone else) and, therefore, might never have evolved as I did.

The financial cost of not treating mental illness includes damaged and ruined lives that show up as lost worker productivity, alcohol and other drug addiction, physical abuse, violence, and homelessness. But the worst loss is the quality of the lives of those affected, people who live with sadness and dread when there could be joy and vitality.

I found light at the end of the tunnel in successful treatment for my own depression, but it wasn't easy. The journey can be difficult and take a long time—sometimes years—to find the medicine or combination of medicines that work best as well as talk therapy with a professional. My long-term psychotherapy was possible only because, in those days (1980–2000), insurance paid for most of it. It frightens me to think how my life might have been without the insurance that allowed me to receive the care that made me well. Should the deep, dark depression ever come again, I know to seek professional help. I've trained myself to be extremely proficient at recognizing the early symptoms.

Anyone who experiences the suicide of a loved one or any trauma should come to some sort of inner peace and reach total forgiveness. You cannot afford *not* to forgive—it's simply too much baggage to carry around. You must find ways to transcend the tragedy and discover peace. Remember the advice of the dying Morrie Schwartz in Mitch Albom's *Tuesdays with Morrie*, "Forgive everyone for everything, now." And that should include yourself.

In addition to professional care, I found I needed to seek my own antidotes for healing. When nothing else worked, I simply put one foot ahead of the next and prayed that better days were ahead. I had to confront the haunting demons of the suicides, de-mystify them, and change what seemed to be a rock-hard beast of sadness into dust.

The difference between a good life and a bad life can be as simple as a tiny pill to balance brain chemistry and circuitry. For some, finding the right medicine can literally make the difference between life and death. I ponder that sobering thought sometimes as I take my anti-depressant, nefazondone, that costs me about thirty dollars a month (and my insurance company an equal amount).

I've learned that the strange darkness that can come from seemingly nowhere, which flows into my psyche, is not something to fear. I know this animal, this beast. I know it will not last forever, and I know there are immediate things I can do to try and break the cycle. I increase exercise, call friends, do something that stirs my mind to distract the gloom. As I learned to pay close attention to my moods, I was astonished at the ease with which I so adroitly recognized the slightest hint of symptoms, took action, and often changed my perspective.

I learned to go out of my way to seek experiences that stimulated and nourished my mind and spirit. A talk by Stephen Hawking in Seattle filled my head with new ideas that I didn't fully understand but surely expanded my thinking. As I drove home, I thought, *Clever me, I've learned to push sadness to the back seat ... for a while.*

Even Virginia Woolf, who committed suicide, wrote in *Mrs. Dalloway*, "Health is largely a matter of our own control. Have I lost the things that matter? What makes us go on? There are certain times in our lives that we want to stay, stay, stay."

Marcel Proust wrote in *Swann's Way* that Swann's depression was "followed by a sort of spiritual overflowing ... [an] enrichment of his inner life." *Now, that's good news.*

I began to see a future with new paths and asked myself each day what I could do to move forward. In the worst of my agony, there was a subtle point of change, some unconscious summing up. A threshold was crossed, and I knew I would never return to that depth of remorse again. My mind pulled together the understanding to seal, at last, the peace in my soul that I had been struggling to attain. The suicide beasts were as tame as they had ever been.

My talk therapy was as important as medicine to my success. While medications may help a depressed person, talk therapy, with or without medicine, can be of tremendous value. It certainly was for me. By continually trying to understand myself, I literally saved my life. It was my work in the end, but my doctor was crucial. How can insight and change *not* occur if someone talks and talks until the bad beasts are tamed? I needed a listener who was detached, and he was.

While a depressed person can't just snap out of it, there is a role that attitude can play. It takes courage to fight depression. Positive thinking, the nemesis of anyone depressed, also helps tilt the scale towards success. I read in *Heather's Rage* by Leslie Byers about a Chinese saying, "To conquer the beast, one must first make it a friend." I liked that and vowed to keep searching for solutions for as long as it took.

Nell Casey in *Unholy Ghost: Writers on Depression*, wrote, "Now I think of depression with curiosity rather than fear. I know that it will not last."

I tried to picture myself down the road in another frame of mind where I might be happy, and that drove my determination and gave me courage to confront the pain. I developed new perspectives where I learned to believe in a life of peace and happiness.

In the worst of it, I felt disconnected from hope. That's when I had to stare in the mirror and rally all the allies in my soul, all the energy in my body, all the rage of defiance in the world against the ugly sadness that I know is *not* a permanent state. I decided to trust that positive changes would emerge over time. I had to… because the alternative was unthinkable.

INSIGHT FROM A MEDICAL PROFESSIONAL

In 2004, I tracked down and interviewed Jerry Rosenbaum, one of a couple of friends in Curt's hotel room when Dad and I committed him to the psychiatric hospital. I found him at Harvard's Medical School, serving as chief of psychiatry at Massachusetts General Hospital.

"Hello Jerry. Thanks for agreeing to meet with me."

"Certainly. If I can be of any help, I'm most happy to tell you what I remember."

"I recently realized that it was twenty-five years ago, almost to the week, when I last saw you. So, when did you meet my brother?"

"I met Curt sometime in the mid-seventies, and we got together socially several times. Curt was hilarious, creative, quite bright, and a joy to be with. And then some months later, things changed; I got a strange call from him telling me to avoid a particular man because he carried a gun. The next thing I remember is that he called saying he needed a psychiatrist because he was going to run for mayor of Boston. I said, 'Oh, that sounds crazy,' and he said, 'That's why I need a psychiatrist to convince people that I'm not crazy.' That's when he was holed up in the Parker House hotel after his finances and business had tumbled. But, because he was my friend, I was concerned, so I went to the hotel where I found him clearly manic and psychotic. At that point, it was pretty clear that he was at least bipolar and committable to a psychiatric hospital.

"After he was released from the hospital, he went on this odyssey of homelessness, and some time passed, months and then years. Then he contacted me and detailed how he'd gone from town to town and how he was traumatized in some places as a vagrant. When I saw him after his homeless period, he was almost unrecognizable. He just didn't look like the same person—he'd lost a lot of weight, and his face was gaunt. I had phone calls from him from a number of different places, and he came to see me a few times for lunch. He wanted to figure out why he'd been put on medicine. He never felt that he'd been ill. He wanted to talk about his sometimes unusual and elaborate theories about all kinds of things. I remember regretting that, unlike a lot of people who have manic episodes, he didn't have restitution. That means in contrast to more progressive disorders like schizophrenia, people with bipolar illness—at least in the early years of the illness—typically have pretty clear restitution to well-being between episodes, in contrast to schizophrenia, where people often continue with residual symptoms after a psychotic episode. But Curt clearly was still a little nutty even though he wasn't manic—so that was not a good prognosis. That means he could have been diagnosed as schizoaffective, as opposed to pure bipolar, because he still had paranoid ideas. He also had lots of theories about how the brain worked, accounting for neurologic and psychiatric symptoms and syndromes and why other people didn't understand his genius. At those times, he wasn't overtly manic, but quite calm."

"What do you make of the fact that Curt was always in denial about his illness?"

"That's pretty typical of mania. It's a brain state where people lack insight; they can't see themselves as others do but rather look like they are denying the obvious. It's analogous to a condition you see sometimes after strokes called anosognosia. Some people paralyzed after a stroke are asked, 'Can you move your arm?' and they say, 'Yes.' They are not deliberately trying to mislead but just have a lack of awareness that is not altered by the evidence. Yet, the doctor knows, from a brain scan for example, that they can't, but they still deny anything is wrong. There's something about mania—even when people are completely nuts—that people fail to see these deficits or behaviors clearly. It's not as if they are pretending, denying, ashamed, or not wanting to admit;

it's a real inability to see. I think for many people, it's part of the illness. Sometimes after people do have restitution, when they're well, they'll say, 'You know, I must have been out of my mind, but at the time, it didn't seem that way.' For others, even in retrospect, they come up with explanations to justify bizarre behavior and continue to lack insight. People just can't see it, as obvious as it is to others. The circuits aren't functioning to allow that kind of recognition.

"I had a patient picked up by the police walking naked along the highway. Even months later, the individual came up with an explanation that seemed reasonable and said that people over reacted. The anosognosia is not a universal complication of mania, but I've seen it enough to think that it's part of being manic—that loss of judgment is one symptom of that same inability to self-monitor."

"That's very interesting and helpful. Thank you. Through the years, I was with Curt during his bouts of mania, depression, and craziness. I always doubted his conspiracy theory but, at the same time, didn't want to believe that he was crazy. If there were even slivers of truth in his stories, I wanted to track them down. If I could prove that some of these stories were true, then it would mean that Curt wasn't making everything up and therefore wasn't entirely crazy. I nearly always believed him—after all, he was my older brother—so it was difficult to accept that he might be that crazy. I thought that if he was crazy, well then, what about me? But, I finally realized—thank God—that I am not my brother. Yet I felt compelled to be his final advocate and get to as much truth as I could."

"Curt would appeal to me to be his advocate, too. We had a certain bond, even though he was crazy, even when he thought that I couldn't see what he was seeing—his genius, why there was a conspiracy, his theories about all kinds of things. He had lots of ideas. I remember listening to him trying to create his own neuroscience, really, and through it all, even when he thought I was skeptical or not understanding, or even a member of the Establishment that had caused him such trouble, I knew there was an element of trust for me, that I was someone he'd come back to.

"In some people, the disorder progresses when they're not treated. In others, it progresses when they are treated. There is evidence that the longer people are sick, the harder it is to recover. The longer you're sick, the more episodes you have, the more you're subsequently going to have. Treatment can shorten and prevent relapse so may influence the course—to some extent—though that's still a little soft in terms of the data to back it up.

"I know at the time when he was about to be acclaimed by popular demand the next mayor of Boston, you would want to do anything you could to avoid hospitalization and get him the right treatment. But I don't think there was an option at that point because his insight was so limited. He certainly would probably have gone on to embarrass himself. Sooner or later, he most likely would have encountered the legal system that would have forced the same outcome, with more embarrassment, cost, or injury along the way.

"It was in some ways too bad I was his friend because it would have been better if I had been his psychiatrist … not that the outcome would have been different.

"I hope this helps you in some way."

"Yes, it has. Thank you very much."

Rainforest Sizzle

I had a dream that I was at the end of a diving board, high on a cliff above a lake in the woods, safely balancing upside down on my head and hands. *Should I dive or not?* I looked down and saw rocky cliffs. *Did I really want to do this?* I felt my legs lean toward the water far below and gravity pulled me to the tipping point. I was frightened by the serious danger. I decided I didn't want to dive into danger, but needed to fight strongly to overcome inertia. I was terribly distressed until I gave my will power full throttle and, like a Superwoman, overcame the odds, and pulled back to safety. At first, I wasn't certain I could save myself; it would be difficult. Then a surge of emotional and physical power made me realize I would survive because I had made up my mind to do so. It was as simple as that.

Now that was a nice dream.

~ ~ ~

I finally decided to track down Curt's long time psychiatrist, Dr. Joseph Nostrum, the man most responsible for Curt's committal. He would be the one most likely to be able to verify or deny the conspiracy theories Curt had always touted. He practiced near Boston and I interviewed him in his office.

Nostrum reported, "I saw Curt unraveling. His judgment was failing; he was becoming grandiose and had an air of dramatic excitement. I became concerned about his grandiosity and suggested hospitalization and, of course, he didn't agree."

I looked Nostrum squarely in the eye and asked if he had ever been part of, or was aware of, a conspiracy against my brother, and he replied, "Absolutely not."

~ ~ ~

After a summer sleeping a total of twenty-seven nights under the stars in my tent, I wrote:

> What have I learned from the peace in the forests, the gushing glacial streams, and the crackling campfires? As I read and write in this haven of heaven, I fine-tune my discernment. I am mesmerized by the slow degeneration of the fiery logs. Every now and then, there is a snap, a sizzle—just like life. Then the tempo slows. To keep the fire vital, it needs feeding and tending—just like life. Have there been enough good snaps and sizzles in my life? What could I, should I, create in my remaining years? From the fire comes warmth and glowing embers and then they diminish and die—transformed into new energy, as we all will be someday. Insight sometimes comes unexpectedly in the most common experiences. Surrounding myself with nature's beauty provides a peace and calmness not found anywhere else. How many more nights shall I have beneath the stars? It is a limited number now, as it always has been, but I've learned to cherish each moment more. My soul is nourished by thankfulness.

On another summer evening, moonlight poured down on me while camping on a cliff above Puget Sound on the Olympic Peninsula. Nestled in my sleeping bag, I heard the last crackling sputters of my campfire and, later, total soundlessness. I fell into a peaceful, timeless sleep. After a while, I heard a faint sound in the still night air—something I couldn't identify. Slowly and steadily advancing with increasing power and volume, I realized it was the tide coming in as I heard the waves wash gently on the shore. I felt their power, their relentlessness. These waves are forever; nothing will ever stop them. *Now, there's an immutable anchor.*

I imagine most people have certain places, especially in nature, where they feel awed and empowered. It's like an access point to your soul. They are places where one finds something powerfully life-giving, connecting spiritually with nature.

Billy Marshall Stoneking, author of the play about Ezra Pound, *Sixteen Words for Water*, writes of "those special, personal places; not special by chance, but because we find parts of ourselves in them, and leave parts of ourselves behind. Places full of power. Sacred places. Places where one feels a contentment, a belonging; where one feels whole."

Being in nature, the rhythms of my body find balance, stability, and empowerment, linking to the energy in the water, woods, and wind which I tap into and feel great joy with the connection. These quiet experiences cleanse my soul. The trees, plants, and earth serve as conduits and provide grounding energy. I reveled in Beauvoir's words from *All Said and Done*, "Despite all the deaths that lay behind me … I had reestablished myself in the condition of happiness. Of all the blows I had endured, none had broken me."

~ ~ ~

Two years after my introduction to Kwan Yin, I returned to Cloud Mountain for another meditation and writing retreat with Sandy Boucher. I was in the meditation hall, nestled among tall pines in a rainforest, sitting on the floor with about thirty people. We were each asked to bring an object of significance to share. When it was my turn, I held up a postcard of the Kwan Yin statue in Kansas City and suddenly gasped. My heart quickened and eyes widened.

"Oh my. This is amazing! I just had an epiphany as I looked at the orange in this postcard. At this moment, I've realized some connections between experiences I've had … all tied to this vibrant orange color here in the photo. It's the same orange of a moonset I saw last summer and the same orange of my brother's hair and the same orange on the dead robin's breast and the same orange of the exploding lava on my wall calendar."

The moonset epiphany brought me more deeply connected to life. But the story's not over.

Fish Monsters Captured

Through the purple and sulfur sky, I felt happy... on the other
side of a line that I could never turn and recross again ...
The sky is not so heavy any more. A page has been turned
and I can attempt to sum up.

—Simone de Beauvoir, *Force of Circumstance*

Five years after Curt's suicide and nine years after Dad's, two new monsters appeared in a dream. I was in the back shop of our newspaper where half a dozen people were working. As publisher and manager, I was smiling and pleased things were running smoothly. I moved to another part of the shop where several men were standing around a large rectangular hole in the floor where the hatch door to the basement was open.

I looked down and was startled to see not the press room but dark and foreboding murky water—like India ink—sloshing wildly to and fro. The frightening energy in the waves showed there had been recent torment. Then I saw on the floor, next to the men, two large, black and slimy primordial fish-like creatures that had been pulled from the murky depths. They were a strange confluence of mammal and fish with the mass of good-sized harbor seals. They were motionless and dead, having been captured from the waters below.

The men in the shop who retrieved the demons were happy and joyful. We all shared a great sense of relief and came to the same conclusion: the future would surely be better because of this. I heard footsteps and turned around; there was Dad, in his mid-seventies, who had come in the back door. His thick gray hair was nicely groomed and he looked fresh and perky in a plaid shirt as he walked briskly through the shop. He said not a word, but smiled broadly and gave me a strong nod of approval.

I awoke with an immensely happy aliveness. I knew immediately that the two creatures in the murky waters were Curt and Dad's suicides. The monsters had been caught, exposed, and removed. My fear was gone, and I shouted for joy.

~ ~ ~

On a warm and lovely fall day with a pristine, cobalt sky, I went to my deck to read. As the sun warmed my face, my mind drifted into a meditative state, and I felt a pleasant energy flow into my body.

I like the way I've learned to get over things with ease and not let them disturb my equanimity. Anita Diamant's words in *The Red Tent* resonated with me, "Do not let the hurts of the past cling to you." I don't let blimps be floodgates to past sorrows anymore. *I like this sense of a firm foundation so I'm not a bleeding lamb when things don't go right.* I realized I was capable of extremely healthy behavior. My muse was calm and content and I was making my way.

I thought of Martin Luther King's words, "[There are times in our lives when] there are those moments of unutterable fulfillment which cannot be completely explained by those symbols called words. Their meanings can only be articulated by the inaudible language of the heart."

As my book neared completion, I spent a few hours with Sandy Boucher and talked through my book, chapter by chapter. When I got to the part about the orange connection, her eyes became wide.

"Well, that's very interesting because there is, as you may recall from my *Discovering Kwan Yin* book, the ancient Chinese full-moon meditation. We probably did it at the retreat. You imagine you're on the beach, and the moon starts coming down toward the water. As it comes down, you realize Kwan Yin is standing in the moon. She then moves towards you and merges with you. It's about opening yourself to compassion."

"Oh my goodness, Sandy. That's amazing! So the moonset that was such a powerful and vivid experience to me is something people have been experiencing for thousands of years?"

Her eyes twinkled and she grinned broadly, "Well, yes. I suppose you could say that. See, it's getting more complex."

I went home and pulled out my copy of *Discovering Kwan Yin*, which I had read years ago when I had first met Sandy. Sure enough, in the back of the book was a meditation where you imagine yourself by the ocean with a full moon glistening on the water. Here are excerpts:

> Gradually, the moon becomes Kwan Yin herself, her body surrounded by a glowing aureole. Slowly, she descends towards you ... As she comes closer, let her radiance enter you. Let her strength, her peace, her compassion become a part of you. Let yourself open to her so that she merges completely with you.

I recalled my night camping when I awoke to the bright orange moonset, keenly aware that something powerful and positive had happened but not knowing what.

Now, I knew. It was the Buddhist goddess Kwan Yin with her thousand arms and thousand eyes who wrestled me from sleep that night to bring me peace.

Timothy Eagan, in *The Good Rain*, quotes Theodore Winthrop's journal of 1853, "Studying the light and the majesty [of Mount Rainier], there passed from it and entered into my being, to dwell there evermore ... a thought and an image of solemn beauty, which I could thenceforth evoke wherever in the world I must have peace or die."

In my life, I have bounteous memories of witnessing nature's beauty, akin to Winthrop's, and I also have the memory of dancing in the sun the day I learned my brother's death was suicide. Now, there's no doubt in my mind that it was his spirit who helped pull me into the folk dance that day.

Curt always wanted his words to be read by others, so here's my humble homage to his life and dreams... and I am left with my soul evolved.

Epilogue

Ten years after Curt's death, I saw Ted Sorensen on C-SPAN's *Book TV*, discussing his new tome and final tribute to John F. Kennedy, *Counselor*. Sorensen, then eighty, was as sharp and adroit as ever. As I heard the rich detail come forth in his stories, I decided the time had come. I would do something I'd thought about for thirty years: I'd write Sorensen a letter and ask if he remembered Curt. Around the time Curt was at the peak of his career, he had done some work for Sorensen. Curt would talk about him with great admiration, highly extolling the man's abilities and eloquence. So, I wrote Mr. Sorensen:

> Greetings from a fellow Nebraskan.
>
> When you were starting law school in Lincoln, I was twenty-five miles west cutting my baby teeth on wood type at my father's newspaper office, *The Seward County Independent*. My father, Henry Mead, owned the paper from 1949–1977, and I served as publisher from 1972–1975.
>
> I'm writing to ask if you have any recollections of my red-haired brother, Curt Mead, which you might share with me for a book I'm writing. Curt died in 1998, a suicide, after battling years of mental illness.
>
> Curt did some political consulting work for you sometime between 1971 and 1978 when he lived in New York and Boston.
>
> Sincerely,
> Evonne Agnello

A few days later, an e-mail arrived from Mr. Sorensen:

> Dear Mrs. Agnello,
> I remember your brother well, but sadly. He was a very bright and energetic assistant on a political assignment in the 1970s, and I liked him and his colleague very much. His illness became apparent to me in time—apparent because of my own experience with my mother as discussed in my new book. I never saw Curt after that, which may have been just as well inasmuch as he was writing me, threatening to kill me unless I paid him the $1 million he said I owed him. At one point, my secretary contacted your father, if I recall correctly. That is a sad story but he was certainly a bright and likeable young man before his illness. My heart goes out to his family.
> Sincerely,
> TCS

> Dear Mr. Sorensen:
> Your thoughtful note brought some sorrow but, more important, healing. I was not aware Curt had threatened to kill you.
> For nearly twenty years, Curt claimed that his hospitalization was the result of a conspiracy and not mental illness. When he died, I vowed to track down what slivers of truth I could. There was no question he had serious mental illness, but because I loved him dearly as my brother and wanted to give him the benefit of the doubt, I was resistant to believe he would be *that* ill.
> Now, my few lingering thoughts about the possibility of some truth to Curt's conspiracy stories have been put to rest. I will always be grateful to you for this. I was touched by the story of your mother's mental illness in *Counselor*. Curt spoke so fondly of you for many years.
> Sincerely,
> Evonne Agnello

Sorensen's note arrived on a day when I was camping in the Olympics and had gone into Forks to check my e-mail. That evening, under a glistening full moon, mirrored on the Hoh River, my mind grappled with the new information and I wrote:

> Today, all lingering thoughts about the possibility of some truth to Curt's stories were put to rest at last. The final nail was driven into the absolute proof that Curt's mental illness was serious. Of course, I knew that before, but Sorensen's compelling

story was a way for me to finally close my thirty-year quest for the truth. I've come to believe that Curt had an unhealthy brew of bad luck, bad choices, and untreated mental illness.

I can say with surety now that there was no conspiracy against my brother, yet his illness allowed him not only to imagine it but also believe it for twenty years.

Acknowledgements

"Great writing matters and has the potential to change the world," so saith David Guterson. In 2002, that belief drove him and Nichole Vick to co-found Field's End, a 100-percent volunteer organization that has provided professional-quality writing classes for the past ten years.

I am one of the many benefactors of those efforts and thank Field's End for providing volunteer opportunities and outstanding classes and conferences that sharpened my skills. Field's End is a model any community could adapt. Think of a world where people would write clearly ... and the ramifications of that on everything.

Living in Puget Sound, I am blessed with a plethora of opportunities to hone my writing skills and hear authors. I've been inspired by authors at The Seattle Arts and Lectures Literary Arts Series, programs by Tacoma's Public Library, the Seattle 7 Writers, and our iconic and beloved Elliott Bay Bookstore, where they have three authors speaking *every single day.*

I also took writing classes at Tacoma Community College, Richard Hugo House, the Pacific Northwest Writers Association, and Cloud Mountain Retreat Center. Outstanding instructors at Hugo House included John Marshall, former *Seattle Post-Intelligencer* book critic, and author Rebecca Brown. And, bravo to Sheryn Hara, for successfully resurrecting Seattle's Northwest BookFest in 2011. This fest has inspired me and thousands of others to read books and write.

And, here's a big salute to Steve Scher, a huge promoter of books and an astute interviewer of many authors on his thought-provoking show, *Weekday*, on Seattle's NPR affiliate KUOW, 94.9 FM. My knowledge of authors and books has grown immensely over the years from C-SPAN's Book TV, forty-eight hours of non-fiction book programs each weekend. I am grateful for the expert guidance of Dr. Dianna Marre, who for several years, taught classes on memoir writing at Tacoma Community College. After I took it a few times, she pulled me aside and firmly proclaimed, "You have the makings of a great book here; you *have* to do this, Evonne." Her confidence buoyed me forward. I also want to thank Buddhist author Sandy Boucher, one of the most evolved women I know. From her, I learned Vipassana meditation, which has helped me develop peace, clarity, a sense of well-being, and improved writing.

Working as a volunteer at the 2011 Northwest BookFest, I met Sheryn Hara of Book Publisher's Network and immediately felt she was the one to publish my book, and my intuition served me well. Her team of experts: editor, Julie Scandora, book designer, Stephanie Martindale, and cover designer, Laura Zugzda, provided outstanding service.

Across the seas to Australia, I send my gratitude to the talented poet, playwright, and author, Billy Marshall Stoneking, for his blessing to reproduce excerpts from his play, *Sixteen Words for Water*. My thanks also to Jim Fulkerson, the actor who played Ezra Pound in Stoneking's play, and Scot Whitney, managing artistic director at Harlequin Productions, State Theater in Olympia.

In my hometown of Seward, Nebraska, I thank Clark Kolterman, who made arrangements for my first reading there, and also the Seward Public Library, the Seward Arts Council, and the Seward Women's Club for sponsoring the event. Special thanks to Kevin Zadina, publisher of the *Seward County Independent*, for his story, "Book to chronicle mental illness."

I'm indebted to many who read parts or all of my book prior to publication: Marjane Ambler, Jennie Borchert, Jeanette Coufal, Sally Craig, Sharon Dotzler, Lowell Erickson, Kay Green, John and Linda Helland, Nancy Hungerford, Carolyn Kelly, Judy Peysar, Nancye Pierce,

Dennis Quinn, Kathleen Rutledge, Barbara Simon, Barbara Williams, Dianne Wright, and Trix Wyant.

I offer special thanks to Dr. Jerry Rosenbaum and Dr. Mark Murphy for their contributions. On the tenth anniversary of Curt's death, I Googled his name and was surprised to find a full page about him in a book, *Heinz Kohut: The Making of a Psychoanalyst,* by Charles Strozier. I contacted Strozier, and he directed me to the archives of the Chicago Institute for Psychoanalysis where Curt's original letters to Kohut reside. Curt would be thrilled to know that his writing will dwell forever among Kohut's.

Thanks to Bob Moffat and other Apple Pickers' members (a Macintosh computer user group) for years of speedy and competent help. Thanks also to Rick Wiley at the *Arizona Star,* the Arizona Historical Society, lava photographer Brad Lewis, Mary Holste, Erik Hanberg, Joe Novak, Shirley Blank, Julie Meyers, and Leslie Malo.

And though deceased, I honor my parents, Henry and Evelyn Mead, and brother Curt, who provided me a wonderful family, hardly perfect, but certainly rich with material for a book. And, last but not least, I thank my son, Adam, for all he has given me. I wanted to make certain he had no unanswered questions about the tragedies that befell his uncle and grandfather.

APPENDIX

Books read by Evonne Agnello 2000 and 2001

2000

Tao Te Ching, Lao Tzu

Walden, Henry David Thoreau

Embraced by the Light, Betty J. Eadie

Higher Power, Deepak Chopra

No Greater Love, Mother Theresa

Yesterday I Cried, Iyanla Vanzant

Sacred Journey, Sam Keen

Flow, Mihaly Csikszentmihalyi

Tuesdays with Morrie, Mitch Albom

Simple Abundance, Sarah Ban Breathnach

Something More, Sarah Ban Breathnach

One Day My Soul Just Opened, Iyanla Vanzant

The Bridges of Madison County, James Waller

The Shipping News, Annie Proulx

Money Smart: Secrets Women Need to Know About Money, Esther M.
   Berger

2001

The Red Tent, Anita Diamant

*The Marriage of Heaven and Hell: Manic Depression and the Life of Virginia
   Woolf,* Peter Dally

Noonday Demon, An Atlas of Depression, Andrew Solomon

Darkness Visible, A Memoir of Madness, William Styron

Unholy Ghost, Writers on Depression, Nell Casey

The Measure of My Days, Florida Scott-Maxwell

Writing Down the Bones, Freeing the Writer Within, Natalie Goldberg

On Becoming a Novelist, John Gardner

A Room of One's Own, Virginia Woolf

Personal History, Katharine Graham

The Prime of Life, Simone de Beauvoir

A Transatlantic Love Affair, Simone de Beauvoir

The Elements of Style, William Strunk and E. B. White

Speak, Memory, Vladimir Nabokov

Writing from the Inside Out, Dennis Palumbo

Hidden Spring, Sandy Boucher

Discovering Kwan Yin, Sandy Boucher

Opening the Lotus, Sandy Boucher

Eveless Eden, Marrianne Wiggins

The Seat of the Soul, Gary Zukav

The Purpose of Your Life, Carol Adrienne

Paradise, Toni Morrison

The Seven Spirit Laws of Success, A Guide to Fulfill Your Dreams, How to Know God, Deepak Chopra

Creating Affluence, The A-Z Steps to a Richer Life, Deepak Chopra

The Gift of a Year, Myra Kirschenbaum

The Way of the Wizard, 20 Lessons for Living a Magical Life, Deepak Chopra

The Temple of My Familiar, Toni Morrison

Earth Odyssey, Mark Hertsgaard

Soul Mountain, Gao Xingjian

The Bone People, Keri Hulme

Fierce Invalids Home from Hot Climates, Tom Robbins

East of the Mountains, David Guterson

On Writing, Stephen King

The Greatest Generation, Tom Brokaw

The Dancing Wu Li Masters, Gary Zukav

The Bonesetter's Daughter, Amy Tan

In Dreams Begin Responsibilities, Delmore Schwartz

Bird by Bird, Anne Lamott

Eleanor Roosevelt, Vol. 1: 1884-1933, Blanche Wiesen Cook

Ya Ya Sisters, Rebecca Wells

Gift from the Sea, Ann Morrow Lindberg

Restoring the Earth, Kenny Ausubel

BIBLIOGRAPHY

Albom, Mitch. *Tuesdays with Morrie*. New York: Doubleday, 1997.

Alda, Alan. *Never Have Your Dog Stuffed*. New York: Random House, 2005.

Artaud, Antonin. *Antonin Artaud: Selected Writings*. Edited by Susan Sontag, translated from French by Helen Weaver. Los Angeles: University of California Press, 1988.

Artaud, Antonin. *Artaud Anthology*. Edited by Jack Hirschman. San Francisco: City Lights Books, 1965.

Ascher, Carol. *Simone de Beauvoir: A Life of Freedom*. Boston: Beacon Press, 1981.

Bair, Deirdre. *Simone de Beauvoir, A Biography*. New York: Summit Books, 1990.

Ban Breathnach, Sarah. *Simple Abundance*. New York: Warner Books, 1995.

Barrington, Judith. *Writing the Memoir*. Portland, Oregon: The Eighth Mountain Press, 1997.

Beauvoir, Simone de. *The Prime of Life*. Cleveland: World Publishing, 1962.

Beauvoir, Simone de. *She Came to Stay*. New York: World Publishing, 1954. First published in Paris by Librairie Gallimard under the title, L'Invitee.

Beauvoir, Simone de. *A Transatlantic Love Affair*. New York: New Press, 1998.

Beauvoir, Simone de. *A Very Easy Death*. New York: G. P. Putnam's Sons. Translated from the French by Patrick O'Brian. First American Edition, 1966. Copyright 1964 by Librairie Gallimard.

Beauvoir, Simone de. *Adieux, A Farewell to Sartre*. New York: Pantheon Books, 1984. Translated from the French by Patrick O'Brian.

Beauvoir, Simone de. *All Said and Done*. New York: Putnam, 1974. Translated from the French by Patrick O'Brian.

Beauvoir, Simone de. *Force of Circumstance*. New York: G. P. Putnam's Sons, 1964. Translated from the French by Richard Howard.

Beauvoir, Simone de. *Memoirs of a Dutiful Daughter*. Cleveland: World Pub. Co., 1959. Translated from the French by James Kirkup.

Beauvoir, Simone de. *The Mandarins*. Cleveland: World Pub. Co., 1956. Translated from the French by Leonard M. Friedman.

Boucher, Sandy. *Discovering Kwan Yin*. Boston: Beacon Press, 1999.

Boucher, Sandy. *Opening the Lotus: a woman's guide to Buddhism*. Boston: Beacon Press, 1997.

Brosman, Catharine Savage. *Simone de Beauvoir Revisited*. Boston: G.K. Hall and Co., 1991.

Byers, Leslie. *Heather's Rage: A Mother's Faith Reflected in Her Daughter's Mental Illness*. Dallas: Brown Books Publishing Group, 2004.

Camus, Albert. *The Stranger*. New York: Knopf, 1946.

Casey, Nell. *Unholy Ghost: Writers on Depression*. New York: William Morrow, 2001.

Chodran, Pema. *When Things Fall Apart: Heart Advice for Difficult Times*. Boston: Shambhala Publications, 2000.

Cisneros, Sandra. *The House on Mango Street*. Houston: Arte Publico Press, 1983.

Collins, Judy. *Sanity and Grace: A Journey of Suicide, Survival and Strength*. New York: Jeremy P. Tarcher/Penguin, 2003.

Conrad, Joseph. *Three Short Novels: Heart of Darkness, Youth, Typhoon*. New York: Bantam Books, 1960.

Cottrell, Robert D. *Simone de Beauvoir*. New York: Frederick Ungar Publishing, 1975.

Cronkite, Kathy. *Conversations About Conquering Depression*. New York: Doubleday, 1993.

Cronkite, Kathy. *On the Edge of Darkness: America's Most Celebrated Actors, Journalists and Politicians Chronicle Their Most Arduous Journey*. New York: Dell Publishing, 1994.

Csikszentmihalyi, Mihaly. *Flow: The Psychology of Optimal Experience*. New York: Harper & Row, 1990.

Dally, Peter. *The Marriage of Heaven and Hell: Manic Depression and the Life of Virginia Woolf*. New York: St. Martin's Press, 1999.

Diamant, Anita. *The Red Tent*. New York: St. Martin's Press, 1997.

Didion, Joan. *The Year of Magical Thinking*. New York: Knopf, 2005.

Eadie, Betty J. *Embraced by the Light.* Placerville, California: Gold Leaf Press, 1992.

Eagan, Timothy. *The Good Rain: Across time and terrain in the Pacific Northwest.* New York: Knopf, 1991.

Evans, Mary. *Simone de Beauvoir: A feminist mandarin.* New York: Methuen, 1985.

Faulkner, William. *As I Lay Dying.* New York: Vintage Books, 1990.

Flaubert, Gustave. *Madame Bovary.* New York: Barnes & Noble Classics, 1948.

Francis, Claude and Fernande Gontier. *A Life, A Love Story: Simone de Beauvoir.* New York: St. Martin's Press, 1987.

Fullbrook, Kate and Edward Fullbrook. *Simone de Beauvoir and Jean-Paul Sartre: The Remaking of a Twentieth Century Legend.* New York: BasicBooks, 1994.

Gardner, John. *On Becoming a Novelist.* New York: Harper & Row, 1983.

Goldberg, Natalie. *Writing Down the Bones: Freeing the Writer Within.* Boston: Shambhala Publications, 1986.

Graham, Katherine. *Personal History.* New York: Vintage Books, 1998.

Guterson, David. *East of the Mountains.* New York: Harcourt Brace & Co., 1999.

Guterson, David. *Our Lady of the Forest.* New York: Knopf, 2003.

Hugo, Richard. *The Triggering Town: Lectures and essays on poetry and writing.* New York: Norton, 1982.

Iyer, Pico. *The Open Road: The Global Journey of the Fourteenth Dalai Lama.* New York: Knopf, 2008.

Jamison, Kay Redfield. *Night Falls Fast: Understanding Suicide.* New York: Knopf, 1999.

Jamison, Kay Redfield. *An Unquiet Mind.* New York: Knopf, 1995.

Jordan, Hamilton. *There's No Such Thing as a Bad Day.* Atlanta, Georgia: Longstreet Press, 2000.

Katie, Byron. *Loving What Is: Four Questions That Can Change Your Life.* New York: Harmony Books, 2002.

Kazantzakis, Nikos. *Zorba the Greek.* New York: Simon & Schuster/Ballantine Books, 1967.

Kazin, Alfred. *Writing Was Everything.* Cambridge: Harvard Press, 1995.

Keen, Sam. *Sacred Journey: Your quest for higher meaning.* New York: Simon & Schuster Audio, 1996.

King, Stephen. *On Writing: A memoir of the craft.* New York: Scribner, 2000.

Kirschenbaum, Myra. *The Gift of a Year.* New York: Dutton, 2000.

Lamott, Anne. *Bird by Bird.* New York: Pantheon, 1994.

Marks, Elaine. *Critical Essays on Simone de Beauvoir.* Boston: G.K. Hall, 1987.

Palumbo, Dennis. *Writing from the Inside Out.* New York: John Wiley & Sons, 2000.

Pipher, Mary. *Seeking Peace.* New York: Riverhead Books, 2009.

Pirandello, Luigi. *Six Characters in Search of an Author.* New York: Dutton, 1922.

Proust, Marcel. *Swann's Way: Remembrance of Things Past.* New York: Vintage Books, 1981.

Pynchon, Thomas. *Deadly Sins.* New York: William Morrow, 1993.

Sambhava, Padma. *The Tibetan Book of the Dead.* Translated by Robert A. F. Thurman. New York: Bantam Books, 1994.

Schwartz, Delmore. *In Dreams Begin Responsibilities.* New York: New Directions Pub., 1978.

Siegel, Daniel. *The Mindful Brain: Reflection and attunement in the cultivation of well-being.* New York: Norton, 2007.

Solomon, Andrew. *The Noonday Demon: An Atlas of Depression.* New York: Scribner, 2001.

Sorensen, Ted. *Counselor: A Life at the Edge of History.* New York: Harper, 2008.

Stegner, Wallace. *Angle of Repose.* New York: Penguin Books USA, 1992.

Stegner, Wallace. *Crossing to Safety.* New York: Random House, 1987.

Stryon, William. *Darkness Visible.* New York: Random House, 1990.

Thruston, Zora Neale. *Their Eyes Were Watching God.* New York, Perennial Library, 1990.

Tolstoy, Leo. *Anna Karenina.* New York: Viking, 2001.

Tzu, Lao. *Tao Te Ching.* Translated by Stephen Mitchell, New York: Harper Collins, 1988.

Van Praagh, James. *Healing Grief.* New York: Dutton, 2000.

Van Praagh, James. *Talking to Heaven: A medium's message of life after death.* New York: Dutton, 1997.

Vanzant, Iylanya. *One Day My Soul Just Opened Up.* New York: Fireside, 1998.

Williams, Terry Tempest. *Refuge.* New York: Pantheon, 1991.

Williamson, Marianne. *Imagine What America Could Be in the 21st Century: Visions of a better future from leading American thinkers.* Emmaus, Pennsylvania: Daybreak, 2000.

Woolf, Virginia. *Mrs. Dalloway.* New York: Harcourt, 1925.

Woolf, Virginia. *A Room of One's Own.* New York: Harcourt, 1957.

Woolf, Virginia. *To the Lighthouse.* New York: Harcourt, 1927.

Yalom, Irvin. *When Nietzche Wept.* New York: Basic Books, 1992.

Zinsser, William, editor, and Russell Baker, Jill Ker Conway, Annie Dillard, Ian Frazier, Henry Louis Gates, Jr., Alfred Kazin, Frank McCourt, Toni Morrison, and Eileen Simpson. *Inventing the Truth: The Art and Craft of Memoir.* Boston: Houghton Mifflin, 1987.

Zukav, Gary. *The Seat of the Soul.* New York: Simon & Schuster, 1989.